Enriching English 5

READER

Collins

Enriching English 5

READER

Ritu Pankaj
Shradha Anand

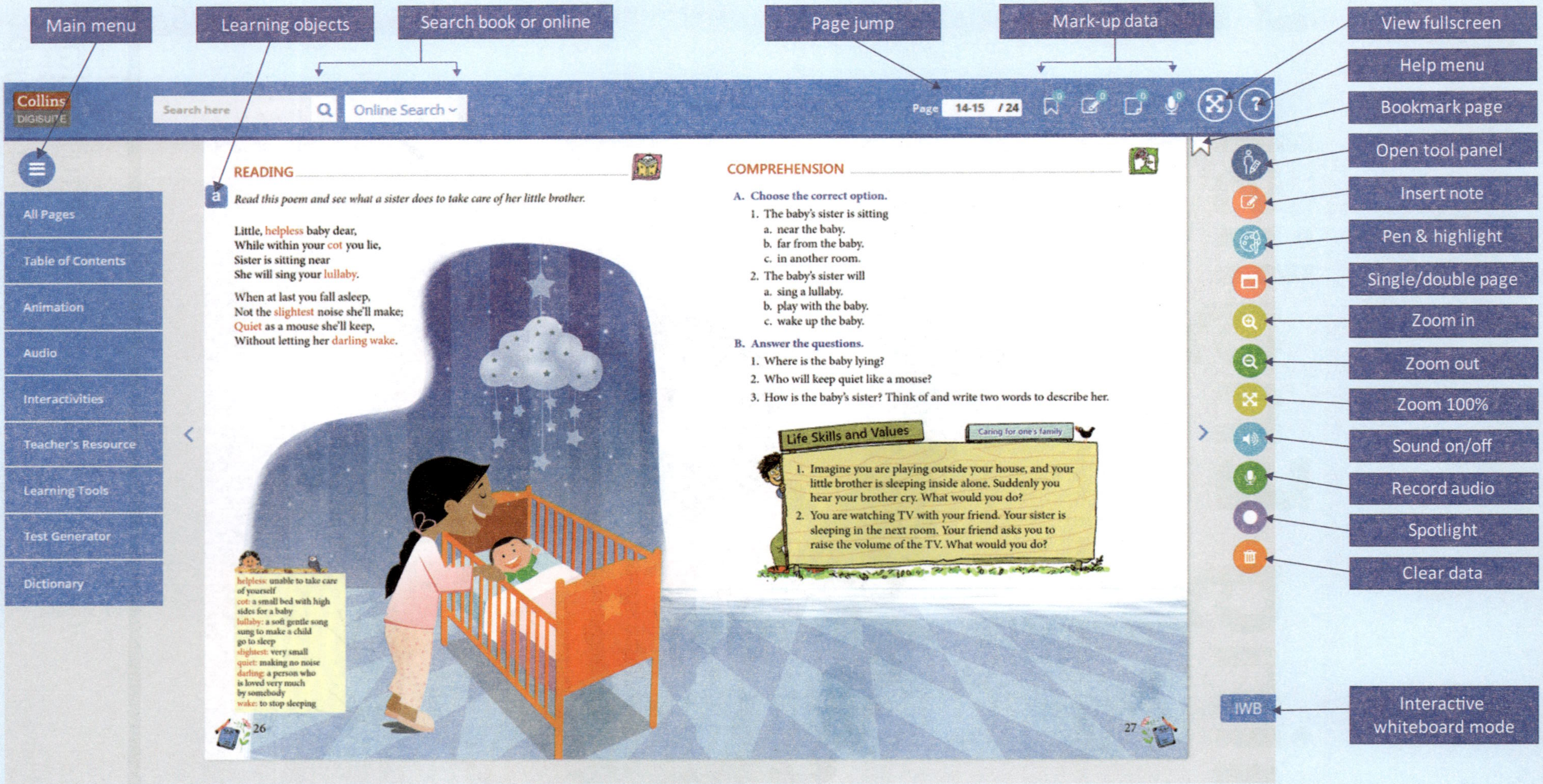

Student + Teacher

- **a** animations
- **ilt** instructor-led tutorials
- **ia** activities
- **w** worksheets
- audio
- **g** games
- **v** videos

Teacher-only

- **lp** lesson plans
- **w** worksheets
- **tn** teacher's notes
- **ak** answer keys

Preface

Literature as an area of study offers a unifying perspective of the world around us. It acts as a prism through which we can view every sphere of human civilization, including history and the sciences.

Enriching English is a language-through-literature course which is designed to introduce students to this larger world through a variety of literary works authored by Indian and global writers. In doing so, it also aims to build the foundations of English language learning by introducing students to the formal structures that enable language acquisition.

The series comprises graded Readers and Language Companions, with support material in the form of Teacher's Resource Books and enhanced digital learning resources.

Readers

The Readers offer a wide variety of engaging literary texts organized thematically. Each unit in the Reader is built around a distinct theme, ranging from family and friendship, to wildlife and outer space. It usually includes a prose and a poetry chapter.

The units begin with **Take Off**, a warm-up section drawn from the theme and related to the reading passages in the units. This section is used for pre-teaching vocabulary to be encountered in the reading passage while drawing on the learner's knowledge of his immediate environment and the larger world. It also includes speaking and writing tasks.

The **reading passages** comprise an eclectic selection of texts, ranging from the classic to the contemporary and include short stories, excerpts from well-known novels, non-fiction passages, poems and plays. They cover a variety of literary genres such as folktale, fable, short story, nonsense poetry as well as extracts from popular novels like *Harry Potter and the Half-Blood Prince*. Each book also includes a graphic story, often a retelling of a well-known folktale, mythological tale or an episode from a novel.

The passages are also interspersed with related trivia in **Food for thought**, and contextual explanations for literary devices and figures of speech in **Literary terms**. Contextually drawn **Common idioms and proverbs**, meant to enhance students' vocabulary, are also covered. A short **biography** introduces students to the author of the passage.

Comprehension includes both factual and inferential questions. Short exercises and 'reference to context' questions check factual understanding of the text. **Life skills and values** includes interpretative and analytical questions which build students' higher order thinking skills while honing their understanding of human values and developing the right attitudes in them.

Vocabulary comprises exercises based on contextual usage and extended word building tasks. It also tests students' understanding of literary devices and figures of speech encountered in the passage.

Grammar includes simple explanations of language structures followed by practice tasks showing graded progression. Tree maps and tables illustrate concepts for easy comprehension.

Study Skills covers the sub-skills of language acquisition and includes phonics and spelling drills as well as dictionary referencing tasks. Special attention is also given to familiarizing students with the use of online dictionaries.

Listening develops aural comprehension skills through various kinds of factual questions.

Speaking covers conversation and role play activities to enable students to respond appropriately in a variety of social situations. It also includes public speaking activities and group discussions.

Writing includes guided and free writing exercises that develop functional and creative writing skills. The **Activity** in the poetry chapters includes exercises which combine hands-on tasks with creative writing skills. Every task includes plenty of scaffolding in the form of suggested vocabulary and reference samples.

Now I can … is a self-assessment checklist for the learner to examine whether they have met the learning objectives for the lesson.

Read at Leisure includes suggestions for further reading related to the author or theme of the reading passage.

Projects, of which there are three, revisit the themes covered in each book. They encourage students to correlate the themes with the world around them through a mix of simple research-based tasks and creative thinking.

A **glossary of literary terms and genres** at the end of the book acts as a ready reference.

Language Companions

The Language Companions complement the Readers. They have been designed to provide practice to the students in the language skills required to excel in the formal examination. They are closely linked to the units in the Reader and cover reading comprehension passages and guided writing tasks besides grammar and vocabulary. The Companions can also act as a self-study tool, providing materials for further practice.

Teacher's Resource Books

The Teacher's Resource Books are designed to facilitate teachers so that they can make the best use of the material given in the books to achieve the objectives set out in the curriculum. They include activity-based lesson plans, additional worksheets on each area of language learning, answer keys to the Readers as well as the listening texts for the aural tasks in the Readers.

Digital Resources

The Collins DigiSuite DVD comprises:

- the Reader given as a **multimedia e-book**, which also includes the complete audio of the reading passages as well as interactive exercises
- **Language Games**, **Pictionary** and a level-appropriate **Collins dictionary** for further practice
- **Test Generator** for quick creation of assignments and test papers
- the **Teacher's Resource Book** in digital format

We hope that this series fosters a love for literature and makes students aware of the many nuances that language lends itself to, while equipping them with the formal language acquisition skills to express themselves correctly in the English language.

Authors

Acknowledgements

The publishers wish to thank and acknowledge the following for granting us permission to use copyright material:

Aaron Shepard for *When the Twins Went to War*. Reprinted with the permission of the author; Janaki Lenin for *Sudan: The End of a Species*. Reprinted with the permission of the author; Paul Perro for *The Labours of Hercules*. Reprinted with the permission of the author; *Ron and the Lucky Potion* from *Harry Potter and the Half Blood Prince*: Copyright © J.K. Rowling 2005; Christopher Merrill for an excerpt from *A Boy Juggling a Soccer Ball* from *Watch Fire*. Copyright © 1994 by Christopher Merrill. Reprinted with the permission of The Permissions Company, Inc., on behalf of White Pine Press, *www.whitepine.org.; Scientific Inquiry* by Susan Blackaby; Copyright © 2014 by Susan Blackaby, from *The Poetry Friday Anthology for Science* by Sylvia Vardell and Janet Wong (Pomelo Books).

The publishers have applied for permission for the following:
Jatin's Sandals by Sukumar Ray; *A Secret for Two* by Quentin James Reynolds; *The Concert* by Shanta Rameshwar Rao; *Art is Hard* by Gareth Lancaster.
Acknowledgements for these texts will be made in the future editions of the book.

Every effort has been made to trace copyright holders and to obtain their permission for the use of copyright material. However, in some instances, we have been unable to trace the owners of the copyright pieces published here. The authors and publishers will gladly receive any information enabling them to rectify any error or omission in subsequent editions.

Cover: MashaStarus/iStockphoto.

Inside Page 13: Pijama61, RobinOlimb; **20:** Andrew_Rybalko; **22:** Primulakat; **26:** Salvadorova; **28:** Page Light Studios, Ljupco, Bartosz Hadyniak; **36:** MedejaJa; **46:** Duncan1890; **47:** Whitemay; **48:** IPGGutenbergUKLtd, Maodesign, Invisiblewl; **56:** Nina_Piankova; **63:** Grandfailure, RobinOlimb; **65:** Patrick Hartung; **66:** Scoobers; **68:** Wrangel; **81:** Clipartdotcom, Good_Stock, Insima, MatiasEnElMundo; **87:** Jemastock; **89:** Blueringmedia; **90:** Tribalium, RobinOlimb, Kovalto1, DanielPrudek, Bubaone, Tinkivinki; **108:** Memoangeles, Blueringmedia; **115:** Msonick; **116:** Tomacco, VasjaKoman; **125:** Pijama61; **126:** Adekvat; **127:** Merfin; **128:** Larryrains; **129:** Askmenow; **130:** Pijama61, Aurielaki; **149:** Sebasnoo, Premiumstock, Bdspn, Lemur4eg, Yasbant Negi/The India Today Group/Getty Images, Sipra Das/The India Today Group/Getty Images, Satish Bate/Hindustan Times via Getty Images, ODD ANDERSEN/AFP/Getty Images; **166:** ALINA, Zaricm; **168:** Renita Colaco, VICTOR HABBICK VISIONS/Science Photo Library/Getty Images; **171:** TopVectors; **184:** Phant, Dr3amer, Lecneo, RapidEye, Rbv, Slav, Tanda_V.

Poster Image: TopVectors, NGvozdeva, Zuhria Alfitra, Sabelskaya.

Key Features

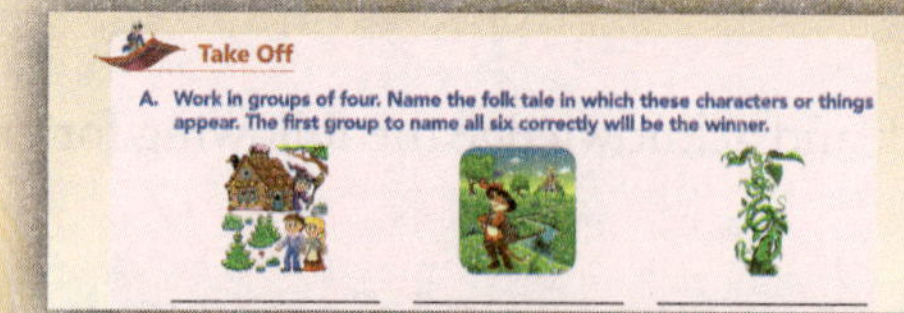
Take Off

A. Work in groups of four. Name the folk tale in which these characters or things appear. The first group to name all six correctly will be the winner.

Take Off has theme-based warm-up activities

Reading

Have you ever looked at the sky and wondered how far away from us the stars are? Though far away, stars brighten the night with their light. Read this poem about the way a small star's light shines far and wide. The first stanza of the poem is a well-known nursery rhyme.

Twinkle, twinkle, little star,
How I **wonder** what you are!
Up above the world so high,
Like a diamond in the sky.[1]

When the **blazing** sun is gone,
When he nothing shines upon,
Then you show your little light,
Twinkle, twinkle, all the night.

In the dark blue sky you **keep**,
And often through my curtains **peep**,
For you never shut your eye,
Till the sun is in the sky.

So the traveller in the dark,
Thanks you for your tiny **spark**,
He could not see which way to go,
If you did not twinkle so.

Literary term

1. This is a **simile**. The poet is comparing the twinkling star to a bright glittering diamond using the word *like*.

wonder: to think about something
blazing: burning or shining brightly
keep: stay
peep: have a quick look at something in secret
spark: (here) light

Common idioms and proverbs

Reach for the stars: Has anyone ever asked you to 'reach for the stars'? This means to try and achieve a very difficult goal.

31

Reading comprises a rich variety of texts by global and Indian writers

Food for thought, Literary terms, Common idioms and proverbs have additional trivia, explanations of figures of speech, idiomatic structures and proverbs

Glossary includes contextual meanings of difficult words

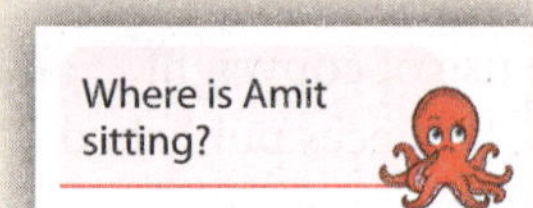
Where is Amit sitting?

While-reading **in-text questions** check factual understanding

About the author/poet includes a brief biography of the author/poet

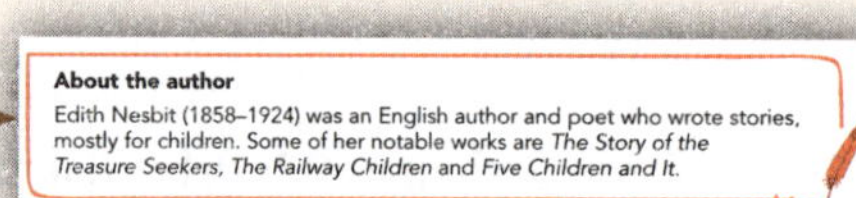
About the author

Edith Nesbit (1858–1924) was an English author and poet who wrote stories, mostly for children. Some of her notable works are *The Story of the Treasure Seekers, The Railway Children* and *Five Children and It*.

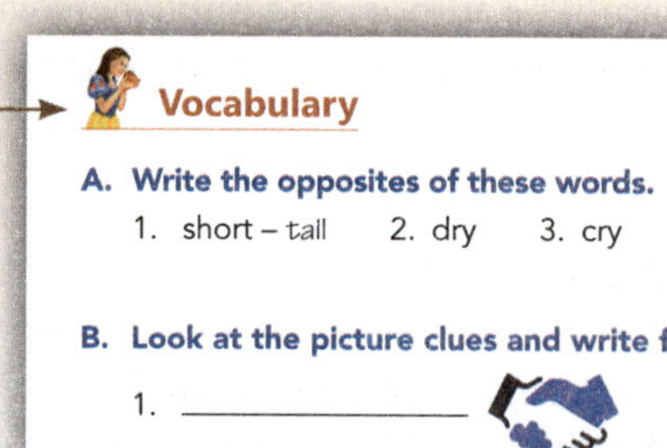
Vocabulary

A. Write the opposites of these words.

1. short – tall 2. dry 3. cry

B. Look at the picture clues and write fo

1. ______________

Comprehension checks factual understanding through 'wh-' and 'reference-to-the-context' questions

Vocabulary includes exercises on contextual usage, modes of vocabulary acquisition and figures of speech

Grammar includes graded practice tasks accompanied by simple explanations

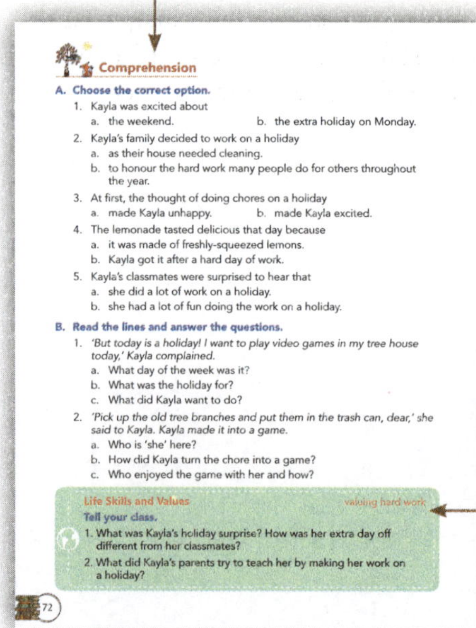
Comprehension

A. Choose the correct option.

1. Kayla was excited about
   a. the weekend. b. the extra holiday on Monday.
2. Kayla's family decided to work on a holiday
   a. as their house needed cleaning.
   b. to honour the hard work many people do for others throughout the year.
3. At first, the thought of doing chores on a holiday
   a. made Kayla unhappy. b. made Kayla excited.
4. The lemonade tasted delicious that day because
   a. it was made of freshly-squeezed lemons.
   b. Kayla got it after a hard day of work.
5. Kayla's classmates were surprised to hear that
   a. she did a lot of work on a holiday.
   b. she had a lot of fun doing the work on a holiday.

B. Read the lines and answer the questions.

1. *'But today is a holiday! I want to play video games in my tree house today,' Kayla complained.*
   a. What day of the week was it?
   b. What was the holiday for?
   c. What did Kayla want to do?
2. *'Pick up the old tree branches and put them in the trash can, dear,' she said to Kayla. Kayla made it into a game.*
   a. Who is 'she' here?
   b. How did Kayla turn the chore into a game?
   c. Who enjoyed the game with her and how?

Life Skills and Values — valuing hard work

Tell your class.

1. What was Kayla's holiday surprise? How was her extra day off different from her classmates?
2. What did Kayla's parents try to teach her by making her work on a holiday?

72

The **Life skills and Values** section has inferential questions on moral values and interpersonal skills.

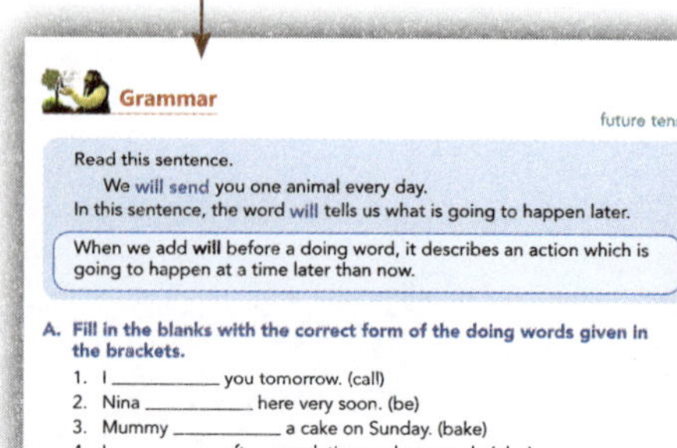
Grammar

future tense

Read this sentence.

We will send you one animal every day.

In this sentence, the word will tells us what is going to happen later.

When we add **will** before a doing word, it describes an action which is going to happen at a time later than now.

A. Fill in the blanks with the correct form of the doing words given in the brackets.

1. I __________ you tomorrow. (call)
2. Nina __________ here very soon. (be)
3. Mummy __________ a cake on Sunday. (bake)
4. I __________ after completing my homework. (play)

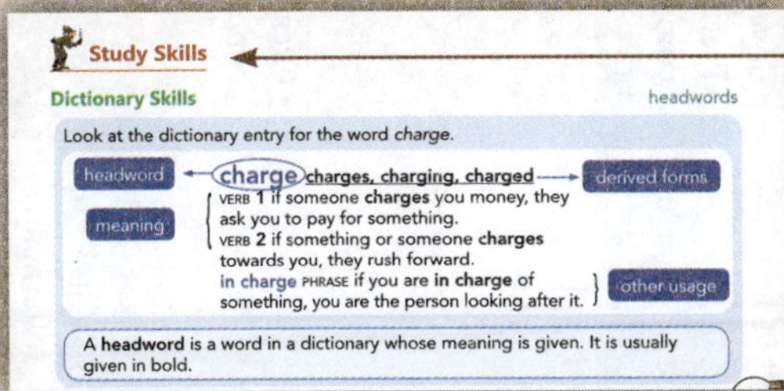

Study Skills includes graded phonics, spelling and dictionary activities

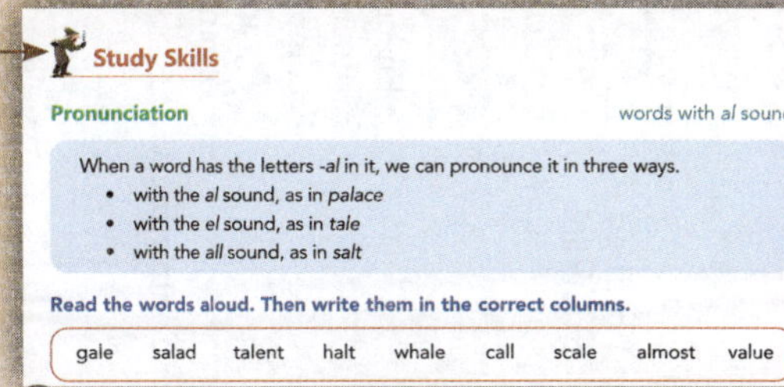

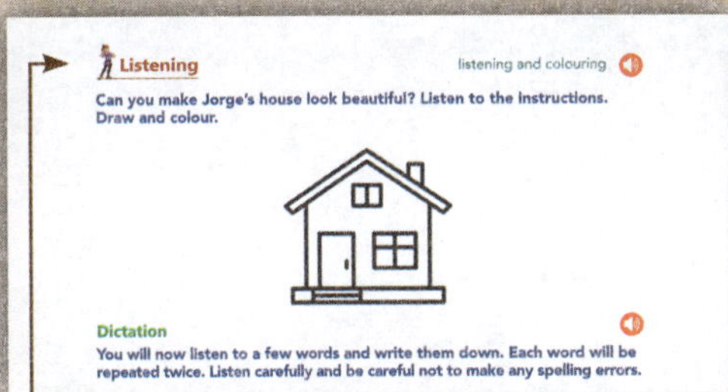

Writing includes graded and free writing tasks. Poetry chapters include **Activity**, a hands-on creative task

Listening covers aural comprehension activities, as well as word and sentence-based **Dictation** tasks

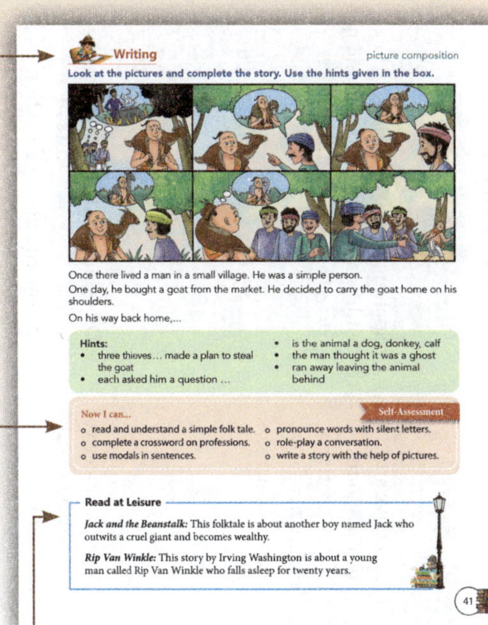

Speaking includes role plays, conversation practice and public speaking tasks through solo, pair and group work

Now I can ... is a self-assessment checklist at the end of every chapter

Cross-curricular **Projects** cover literature-based activities related to the themes in the book

Read at Leisure has suggestions for further reading

Posters explore new categories of literature in every class

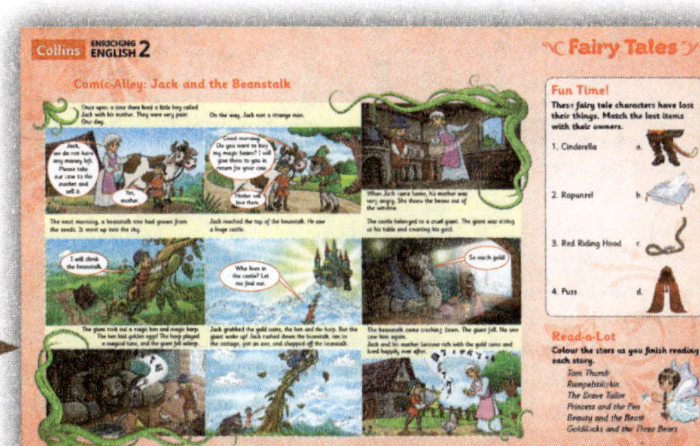

Detailed Contents

Unit	Chapter	Reading comprehension	Vocabulary	Grammar	Study Skills	Listening	Speaking	Writing	Activity
Dreams and Imagination	1. Jatin's Sandals	• Sequencing • Reference to context • Inferential and extrapolative questions	• Words with similar meanings • Suffix *-ly*	• Collective and abstract nouns • Demonstrative and interrogative pronouns	• Spelling: words ending with *-al*, *-el*, *-le*	• Listening to a passage and gap filling	• Narrating a humorous incident	• Writing a paragraph	
	2. Johnny Head-in-Air	• Questions • Reference to context • Inferential and extrapolative questions	• Homonyms						• Enacting situations and completing a graphic organizer
Friendship	3. A Secret for Two	• MCQ • Questions • Reference to context • Inferential and extrapolative questions	• Contextual usage: action words • Analogies	• Types of adjectives • Agreement of subject and verb	• Dictionary Skills: measurement words	• Listening for directions • Dictation	• Conversation: expressing condolences	• Completing a story	
	4. Mary Makes a Friend	• Character study • Questions • Reference to context • Inferential and extrapolative questions	• Contextual usage	• Definite and indefinite articles • Using *some, any, little, few, each, every*	• Pronunciation: diphthongs	• Listening to a poem and answering questions	• Conversation: offering advice	• Writing a diary entry	
Peace and Harmony	5. When the Twins Went to War	• Fill in the blanks • Reference to context • Inferential and extrapolative questions	• Crossword: antonyms	• Adjectives: degrees of comparison • Interjections	• Spelling: error correction	• Listening to a passage and stating true or false	• Conversation: expressing regret and hope	• Writing an essay	
	6. Call for Peace	• MCQ • Reference to context • Inferential and extrapolative questions	• Phrases with 'peace' • Imagery						• Making an origami peace dove • Picture composition
Project 1									
Nature and Conservation	7. Sudan: The End of a Species	• MCQ • Questions • Reference to context • Inferential and extrapolative questions	• Words related to poaching • Phrasal verbs	• Simple and continuous tenses (present and past) • Plural possessives	• Dictionary Skills: speed word search	• Listening to a speech and stating true or false	• Group discussion	• Making a poster	
	8. The Heart of the Tree	• Completing sentences • Reference to context • Inferential and extrapolative questions	• Alliteration • Metaphor						• Creating a concept map
Mythology	9. Phaethon and the Chariot of the Sun	• Flow chart • Reference to context • Inferential and extrapolative questions	• Collocations	• Kinds of sentences • Modals	• Pronunciation: words with *ch* and *th*	• Listening to a story and sequencing	• Role play	• Writing an alternate ending to a story	

	10. The Labours of Hercules	• One-word answers • Reference to context • Inferential and extrapolative questions	• Contextual usage • Same words used as different parts of speech						• Creating an imaginary mythological character
Misadventures	11. Don Quixote and the Enchanted Helmet	• Questions • Reference to context • Inferential and extrapolative questions	• Proverbs • Similes	• Types of adverbs • Conjunctions	• Spelling: words ending with *-er* and *-or*	• Listening comprehension: MCQ	• Role play: enacting a story	• Writing a funny story	
	12. Alone on the Island	• Fill in the blanks • Reference to context • Inferential and extrapolative questions	• Compound words • Suffixes	• Present and past perfect tenses • Punctuation	• Dictionary Skills: guidewords	• Listening to a passage and completing sentences	• Conversation: asking for help	• Writing a message	
Project 2									
Sport	13. Ron and the Lucky Potion	• Sequencing • Reference to context • Inferential and extrapolative questions	• Words related to sport • Homophones	• Direct and indirect speech • Adverbs: degrees of comparison	• Pronunciation: syllables	• Listening to a speech and answering questions	• Giving a speech	• Informal letter	
	14. A Boy Juggling a Soccer Ball	• MCQ • Questions • Reference to context • Inferential and extrapolative questions	• Forming nouns from verbs						• Writing an article
Art and Culture	15. The Concert	• True or false • Questions • Reference to context • Inferential and extrapolative questions	• Forming adjectives from verbs	• Irregular verbs • Prepositions	• Pronunciation: words with *-ea*	• Listening to a passage and answering questions • Dictation	• Conversation: making plans	• Letter writing	
	16. Art is Hard	• Questions • Reference to context • Inferential and extrapolative questions	• Words related to painting • Words of foreign origin						• Writing a report
Science and Technology	17. Nicola Tesla: The Forgotten Inventor	• Fill in the blanks • Reference to context • Inferential and extrapolative questions	• Word search: words related to science • Word families	• Active and passive voice	• Spelling: words with *-able* and *-ible*	• Listening to a passage and gap filling • Dictation	• Interview	• Writing an email	
	18. Scientific Inquiry	• Fill in the blanks • Questions • Reference to context • Inferential and extrapolative questions	• Idiomatic expressions						• Writing a process
Project 3									

Contents

I

Dreams and Imagination

Take Off

A. Do you daydream? Do you think of what you want to do or have when you are older? Write about five such thoughts in the space given.

B. The following people share some common qualities. Write two adjectives to describe them.

1. Sheila does not watch where she is going. Instead, she always looks up at the clouds or at people going by.
2. Rohit's clothes and shoes never last long. His shirts get torn while playing. His shoe straps break soon because he is always in a hurry and never puts on his shoes properly.
3. Suraj daydreams all the time. He thinks of flying planes and visiting new places. He does not hear what the teacher says in class because his mind is always wandering.

1 Jatin's Sandals

Sukumar Ray

Reading

Are you a careful person? Do you handle your books with care and put them away in their proper place after reading them? Read this story to find out what happened to a boy who did not take care of his things.

Jatin's father got him a new pair of sandals and warned him, 'If you tear your sandals this time you shall wear them torn.'

Jatin was a careless boy. He needed a new pair of shoes every month. His clothes always tore after a few days' wear. All his books had torn covers, the pages were **creased**, and his **slate** had a crack from the top to the bottom. Another of his bad habits was to chew the ends of his pencils. They had come to look like groundnut shells[1] because of the constant chewing. When his class teacher saw them, he asked, 'Don't you get proper meals at home?'

Jatin was very careful with his new sandals on the first day after his father's warning. He climbed down the stairs slowly; he crossed the raised door frame carefully so that that he didn't **stumble**. But after a few days, he was his old self again. He rushed down the staircase and stumbled against the stones. Before a month was gone, his sandals were torn along the front.

Literary term

1. This **simile** compares the chewed-on ends of Jatin's pencils to groundnut shells.

His mother advised, 'Call a **cobbler** and get them mended in time, or else they will be finished.' But the cobbler wasn't called and the **soles gaped** wider.

---

creased: marked with lines where pages have been crushed or folded

slate: a square thin sheet of a black rock within a wooden frame, earlier used by school children to write on

stumble: trip and almost fall

cobbler: someone who repairs shoes for a living

soles: the bottom part of shoes

gaped: (here) be wide open

There was only one thing that Jatin cared for—his kite. He would carefully patch and mend any kite that caught his fancy.[2] If the kite had a tear, he'd **barge into** the kitchen demanding glue. If he wanted to add a tail to his kite or needed a pair of scissors, he'd **rummage** through his mother's sewing box. When he was out flying kites he would even forget about his meals!

Common idioms and proverbs

A stitch in time saves nine: This proverb means fixing a problem on time saves a lot of work later. Had Jatin called the cobbler on time, the new shoes might have lasted longer.

What did Jatin love more than anything else?

One day Jatin was rather scared after returning home from school. He had torn his new clothes while climbing a tree. He had tried to push his feet into his sandals, but found them beyond repair. But these thoughts vanished from his mind as he climbed down the stairs to go outside and fly his kite. He jumped down three steps at a time. One sandal **ripped** open so wide that it seemed to **grimace** with all its teeth out.[3] When he jumped over the last three, something strange happened. The ground underneath his feet slid away and his torn sandals whisked him into the sky.

Common idioms and proverbs

2. **caught his fancy:** If something catches your fancy, you like it very much.

Literary term

3. This is an example of **imagery**. The shoe is imagined as a wide-open mouth with the teeth showing.

When the sandals dropped him to the ground, Jatin saw that he had reached a strange place with cobblers sitting all around. When they saw Jatin, they came and took off his shoes and started brushing off the dust carefully. One among them, a kind of leader, said to Jatin, 'I hear that you are very naughty. Look at what you've done to your sandals. They are nearly dead.'

Having regained his **nerve** by then, Jatin asked, 'Does a shoe have a life that you say it's nearly dead?'

'Of course!' the man replied. 'When you run with your shoes on, you think they aren't hurt? That is why they squeak. When you were rushing down the stairs, you **sliced** its sides. That is why you are here. We are in charge of the things that belong to all the boys nearby. When they do not take proper care of their things, we teach them how to.'

The cobbler handed him back his shoes and said, 'Take it! Start mending.'

Jatin was furious. 'I do not mend shoes. Cobblers do that,' he cried.

The cobbler smiled and said, 'It's not so easy to get away, my friend. Here, take the needle and the thread. Start stitching.'

Jatin's anger had **subsided** by then. He felt a little afraid. 'But I don't know how to stitch,' he said. The cobbler replied, 'Don't worry. I will teach you.'

barge into: rush in hurriedly and rudely
rummage: search for something in a hurried way
ripped: tore
grimace: twist one's face in pain
nerve: (here) courage
sliced: cut through
subsided: reduced

The cobbler was patient and Jatin slowly learnt. He had never realised how much skill one needed to mend shoes. The needle pricked his fingers; his neck hurt from bending over the shoes too long. Though he kept at it, after a day's struggle, he had completed only one sandal.

How long did Jatin take to mend the first sandal?

He **pleaded**, 'Can I do the other one tomorrow?'

'What do you mean?' the cobbler said. 'Unless you complete your work, you can't stop. Once you finish the other sandal, you will learn to walk properly so that you don't **torture** your shoes again. Then, you must go to the tailors to stitch your clothes. Then we shall see to the other things that you have broken.'

Tears rolled down Jatin's eyes as he started to repair the second one. Thank god this one wasn't so badly torn.

Next, the cobblers took him to a five-storeyed building. He was made to climb the staircase one stair at a time to the top. If he took more than one stair at a time, he had to come down and start again. Oh, it was hard for Jatin!

Walking slowly now, he reached an open field where tailors sat stitching clothes. Seeing Jatin, they asked, 'What have you torn?' They looked at his ***dhoti*** and shook their heads in **disapproval**. 'Oh, you've torn a good part of this. Sheer **injustice**! Start stitching. Quick.'

Jatin dared not refuse. He took the needle and thread and began to stitch. He had only **pierced** through the cloth twice when the tailors cried, 'Is this what you call stitching? Start over, start over.'

After a while, Jatin begged, 'I am hungry. Take me home. I shall never tear clothes or shoes again.'

The tailors laughed. 'Are you hungry?' they asked. 'We have many of the things you like to eat.'

They brought him some pencils. 'You like to chew pencils, don't you? Eat these, we have nothing else.'

They left him and went back to their work. Tired and hungry, Jatin soon fell asleep. Just then, something swished across the sky.

pleaded: begged
torture: cause great pain
dhoti: a cotton material tied around the waist by men, covering most of the legs
disapproval: dislike for a person or thing, because they may be unsuitable
injustice: lack of fairness
pierced: (here) passed the needle through the cloth

It was the kite that Jatin had **patched**. It whispered to him, 'I have come to help you. You have taken good care of me. Hold on to my tail.'

What two things was Jatin asked to repair in the strange land?

Jatin reached up and held on tightly to the colourful tail of the kite.

They went up into the air with a whoosh. Hearing the sound, the tailors came running. But they could not stop him. He was too high up. Then all of a sudden, Jatin and the kite began to fall out of the sky. Down, down—it seemed as if nothing could stop his fall. Just as he was about to hit the ground, Jatin woke up with a **jolt**. He found himself lying at the bottom of the stairs with a terrible pain in his head. The kite was beside him.

Jatin was ill for a few days. After he recovered, his mother would say, 'Ever since he fell down the staircase, my son has become very weak. He is no longer as energetic. He doesn't rush or jump up and down stairs any longer. How else can his shoes last for four months?'

But the truth was that Jatin had not forgotten the lesson he had learnt from his visit to the land of cobblers and tailors.

(Translated by Zinia Mitra)

patched: (here) repaired by covering a hole with paper
jolt: jerk

About the author

Sukumar Ray (1887–1923) was a poet, writer of short stories, playwright and artist. He was the father of the acclaimed film director, Satyajit Ray. His best known works include *Abol Tabol*, a collection of nonsense poems, *HaJaBaRaLa* and *Pagla Dashu*.

Comprehension

A. Number the sentences to arrange them in the order of events in the story.

- [ ] At first, Jatin was very careful with his new sandals.
- [ ] Jatin's father got him a new pair of sandals and warned him not to tear them.
- [ ] It was the boy's kite which finally rescued him and brought him home.

- [ ] But he soon forgot his father's warning and within a month, tore his new sandals along the front.
- [ ] Here, cobblers and tailors taught him how to mend his torn shoes and shirt.
- [ ] Jumping down the stairs three steps at a time, Jatin slipped and was taken to a strange land.
- [ ] Jatin's mother advised him to get them repaired, but he did not.

B. Answer the questions with reference to context.

1. *'If you tear your sandals this time you shall wear them torn.'*
   a. Who said these lines and to whom?
   b. How did the person spoken to behave after this?
   c. What kind of a boy was this person? How did he keep his books and pencils?
2. *'When they do not take proper care of their things, we teach them how to.'*
   a. Who is being referred to as 'we' and 'they' in the above line? Where were they at the time?
   b. What reason had the speaker just given for shoes making a squeaking sound?
   c. What did the speaker ask the boy to do after saying these words?
3. *'I have come to help you. You have taken good care of me. Hold on to my tail.'*
   a. Who had come to the rescue of the boy?
   b. Why was he ready to help him?
   c. What happened immediately afterwards?

Life Skills and Values — self-discipline, being responsible

1. What are the lessons that Jatin learns in the story?
2. Did Jatin's dream change him into a responsible boy?

Vocabulary

words with similar meanings

Read these sentences.

You like to **chew** pencils. **Eat** these, we have nothing else.
Eat slowly, don't **gobble** your food.
The children **munched** on peanuts.
The words *eat* and *gobble*, and *chew* and *munch* have similar meanings.
But they have small differences.

A. Fill in the blanks with the given options. You may have to make some changes.

1. The tailor did not have the right thread to ___mend___ the tear perfectly. So, he ___patched___ it up as best as he could. (patch, mend)
2. The officer ____________ the envelope with a paper knife and ____________ it open. (tear, slit)
3. This notorious gang ____________ banks and ____________ cash and jewellery. (steal, rob)
4. As the athletes ____________ to the finish line, the crowd ____________ forward to see the winner. (race, rush)
5. Tina ____________ her finger while trying to ____________ a hole in the cardboard. (pierce, prick)
6. He ___________ on the doorstep and ___________ down the stairs. (trip, fall)

suffix -*ly*

B. Fill in the blanks by adding -*ly* to the given words.

real	usual	patient	anxious	quiet	quick

1. The rabbit ____________ jumped into a hole to hide from the hunter.
2. The woman ____________ waited for the bus to arrive.
3. The students read ____________ in the school library.
4. 'Do you ____________ want the job?'
5. 'Did you hear the tiger's roar?' the tourist asked the forest guide ___________
6. I ____________ return home by 6 p.m.

Grammar

collective nouns, abstract nouns

Nouns that refer to groups of people, animals or things are called **collective nouns.**

Examples: The **team** of cobblers and tailors was in charge of things belonging to boys nearby.
Jatin had a loving but strict **family**.

Nouns that refer to things that we cannot see or touch are called **abstract nouns.**

Examples: Jatin's **anger** had subsided by then.
Jatin's stomach growled with **hunger**.

A. Fill in the blanks using the given nouns.

herd	trust	peace	troupe	bouquet	loyalty

1. They presented a ____________ of flowers to the chief guest.
2. I will never break my friend's ____________.
3. She did her job for 35 years and was rewarded for her ____________.
4. The leaders of different countries discussed how to maintain world ____________.
5. The ____________ of dancers will be performing in Russia.
6. The ____________ of buffaloes blocked the street.

demonstrative and interrogative pronouns

Pronouns are words used in place of people or things.

Pronouns that are used to point out specific persons, things or places are called **demonstrative pronouns**. They are *this*, *that*, *these* and *those*.

Examples: **This** is Jatin's house. **That** is his kite.
Eat **these**, we have nothing else.

Pronouns that are used to ask questions are called **interrogative pronouns**. They are *whose*, *what*, *who*, *whom* and *which*.

Examples: **What** have you torn?
Whose are those sandals?

B. Fill in the blanks with the correct pronouns.

1. ____________ should I send the letter to? (whose, whom)
2. ____________ is the book I was talking about. (which, this)
3. ____________ is your favourite colour? (this, which)
4. The workers left ____________ tools on the floor. (these, this)
5. ____________ is the new student in the class? (who, whom)
6. I wonder ____________ knocked on the door. (who, what)
7. Isn't ____________ your coat, the one with the checks? (that, those)

Study Skills

Spelling

words with *-al*, *-el*, *-le*

Look at these words. Some of them are from the story.

stumble **needle** **cobble** **sandal** **squirrel**

These words end with *-le*, *-el*, or *-al*. The pronunciation of these letters are similar and their spelling may sometimes be confused.

Complete the words with *-le*, *-el*, or *-al*.

1. ta __ __	4. rumb __ __	7. med __ __
2. loc __ __	5. cand __ __	8. bubb __ __
3. tow__ __	6. sing __ __	9. trav __ __

Listening

listening for details

Listen to a conversation between two friends about the nature of dreams and fill in the blanks with the correct words and phrases.

1. Lisa dreamt that a stranger was ______________ her and screaming but she could not understand his ______________
2. Garvit dreamt of flying around in a ______________ or being a ______________
3. Lisa dreamt of being a ______________ and telling stories of ______________
4. Most people cannot ______________ in their dreams.
5. Some say that people may dream of things which might ______________

Speaking

narrating a humorous incident

Think of a situation which was difficult at first but later turned out to be funny. It can also be an imaginary situation.

Narrate the incident as humorously as you can within a minute. Use at least two words or phrases from each of the following boxes.

hilarious	ridiculous	amusing
enjoyable	funny	thrilling

squeal	crunch	shriek	thump
sniggered	giggled	clang	rustle

whimper	exclaim	grumble	scream	mumble	joke

storm in a teacup	blue in the face	as cool as a cucumber
spill the beans	grin ear to ear	get cold feet
slip of the tongue	eat like a horse	put one's foot in one's mouth

Writing

writing a paragraph

In the story, Jatin was quick to dismiss the work of a cobbler at first. By the end, he realised that the work of cobblers and tailors is not easy and requires skill and practice.

Using the structure given, write a paragraph on the importance of respecting work of every kind and the people who do them.

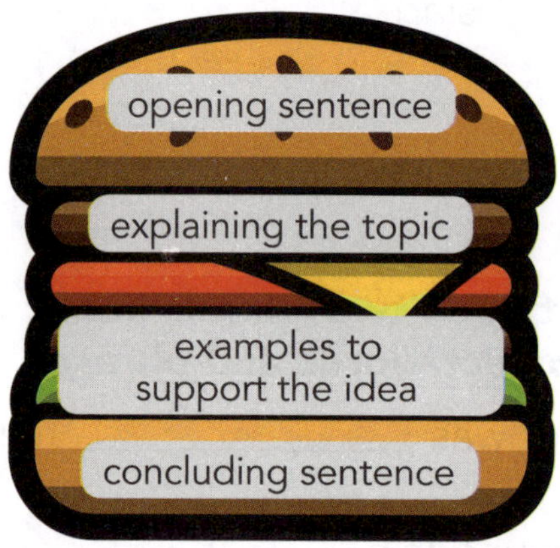

Now I can... **Self-Assessment**

- read and appreciate a story about a boy's carelessness.
- use words with similar meanings and form words with the suffix *-ly*.
- recognize and use collective nouns and abstract nouns, and demonstrative and interrogative pronouns.
- narrate a humorous incident.
- write a paragraph.

Read at Leisure

Magic Moonlight Flower: This magical story by Satyajit Ray is about Sujan, a little boy, who sets out to find a magical flower that will save his father's life.

Pagla Dashu: This collection of hilarious short stories by Sukumar Ray is about the school boy, Dashu, whose crazy ideas and strange actions create excitement and laughter wherever he goes.

narrative poem

2 Johnny Head-in-Air

Heinrich Hoffmann

Reading

Johnny is a curious little boy who has his head up in the air as he explores his surroundings. He has merry little adventures till one big adventure teaches him an unforgettable lesson.

As he **trudged** along to school,
It was always Johnny's rule
To be looking at the sky
And the clouds that floated by;
But what just before him lay,
In his way,
Johnny never thought about;
So that everyone cried out—
'Look at little Johnny there[1],
Little Johnny Head-in-Air!'

Running just in Johnny's way,
Came a little dog one day;
Johnny's eyes were still **astray**
Up on high,
In the sky;
And he never heard them cry—
'Johnny, mind, the dog is nigh!'
Bump! Dump![2]
Down they fell with such a thump,
Dog and Johnny in a **lump**!

Once, with head as high as ever,
Johnny walked beside the river.
Johnny watched the swallows trying
Which was cleverest at flying.

Literary terms

1. This is an example of **alliteration** where the words *look* and *little* are close together and begin with the same consonant sound '*l*'.
2. These are examples of **onomatopoeia**. 'Bump', 'dump' and 'thump' are similar to the actual sounds of a person falling down.

trudged: walked slowly, with heavy steps
astray: away from the correct path
lump: (here) a large heap, without any shape

Oh! what fun!
Johnny watched the bright round sun
Going in and coming out;
This was all he thought about.
So he **strode** on, only think!
To the river's very **brink**,
Where the bank was high and steep,
And the water very deep;
And the fishes, in a row,
Stared to see him coming so.

One step more! Oh! sad to tell!
Headlong in poor Johnny fell.
And the fishes, in dismay,
Wagged their tails and ran away.

There lay Johnny **on his face**
With his nice red writing-case;
But, as they were passing by,
Two strong men had heard him cry;
And, with sticks, these two strong men
Hooked poor Johnny out again.

Oh! You should have seen him shiver,
When they pulled him from the river,
He was in a sorry **plight!**
Dripping wet and such a fright!
Wet all over, everywhere,
Clothes and arms, and face and hair;
Johnny never will forget
What it is to be so wet.

Common idioms and proverbs

The name 'Johnny Head-in-Air' is a play on the phrase '**to have one's head in the clouds**', which refers to someone who is lost in thought or who has plans which cannot actually be carried out.

strode: walked quickly
brink: edge
steep: at a sharp angle
headlong: head first
on his face: with his face on the ground
plight: a dangerous and difficult situation

About the poet

Heinrich Hoffmann (1809–1894) was a German doctor and writer. He wrote many poems, including a collection of illustrated children's verses, which was a Christmas present to his son.

Understanding the poem

A. Answer the questions in a few lines.

1. What was Johnny's 'rule'?
2. Why was he called 'Johnny Head-in-Air'?
3. What were the things which Johnny watched while walking beside the river?
4. Describe the river's brink.
5. What would Johnny never forget?

B. Answer these questions with reference to context.

1. *Johnny's eyes were still astray*
   Up on high/In the sky;
   And he never heard them cry.
   a. What did Johnny not see because his eyes were astray?
   b. What did Johnny not hear?
   c. What happened because of this?

2. *One step more! Oh! sad to tell!/Headlong in poor Johnny fell.*
   And the fishes, in dismay/Wagged their tails and ran away.
   a. Where did Johnny fall and how?
   b. Describe the imagery in the last two lines in your own words.
   c. How was Johnny rescued?

Life Skills and Values — imagination, alertness

1. Do you think Johnny was an imaginative boy? Give reasons for your answer.
2. Was Johnny absent-minded? Give two examples from the poem.

Vocabulary

homonyms

Words that have the same spelling and pronunciation but different meanings are called **homonyms**.

Examples: The river's **bank** was high and steep. (bank = raised grounds along the sides of a river)

Mrs Sharma keeps her precious jewellery in the **bank**. (bank = place where people keep their money)

Complete each pair of sentences with the correct homonyms.

stick | school | face | way | rule | swallow

1. a. According to a new ________, all students have to be in class by 8.30 a.m.
   b. The king will ________ for many years.
2. a. Our ________ gives scholarships to needy students for further studies.
   b. I saw a ________ of fish swim by.

3. a. This is the right ________ to answer the question.
   b. Mini knows the ________ to the library.
4. a. Please ________ the pill with a glass of water.
   b. The ________ is building a nest near our house.
5. a. ________ the photo on the form carefully.
   b. My grandmother is eighty but she can walk without a ________
6. a. Sheena's ________ was shining with excitement.
   b. Since we made a mistake, we have to ________ the punishment.

Activity

enacting situations and completing a graphic organizer

Work in groups of four. Discuss four situations where each of you had your 'head in the air'. What was the consequence of each situation? Did you have to change yourself afterwards? How?
Enact the situations in class and complete the given chart.

Situation	Consequence	How you had to change yourself

Now I can... — Self-Assessment

- enjoy a humorous poem about an imaginative but absent-minded boy.
- use homonyms.
- complete a graphic organizer.

Read at Leisure

Fidgety Phil: This poem by Heinrich Hoffmann is about a little boy who cannot sit still.

M is for Mischief: This collection of fun poems by Linda Ashman is about naughty children and how they cause mischief.

II

Friendship

Take Off

A. Complete the following mind map about your friend.

My friend

- What I like best about him/her
- What I don't like about him/her
- One special thing he/she has done for me
- One special thing I have done for him/her

B. Now look at the following pictures and talk about the different ways in which animals help human beings.

1.

2.

3.

3 A Secret for Two

Quentin James Reynolds

Reading

Some people form strong bonds of friendship, not just with other people but also with animals. Such bonds are based on loyalty and love. Read this story about such a bond between a man and his horse.

For how many years had Joseph drawn Pierre's milk wagon?

Montreal, like all large cities, has some very small streets. No one knew Prince Edward Street as well as Pierre Dupin, for he had delivered milk to the families on the street for thirty years now.

Over the past fifteen years, the horse which drew his milk wagon was a large white horse named Joseph. In that part of Montreal which is very French, the animals, like children, are often given the names of saints. When Pierre had first seen Joseph, he had **stroked** the softness of the horse's neck and looked into his eyes and said, 'This is a kind, gentle and faithful horse and I can see a beautiful spirit shining out of its eyes. I will name him after the good **Saint Joseph**, who was also a gentle and beautiful spirit.'

Within a year Joseph knew the milk route and Pierre used to **boast** that he didn't need reins. Each morning Pierre arrived at the stables of the Provincale Milk Company at five o'clock. The wagon would be loaded and Joseph **hitched** to it.

Pierre would call '***Bonjour***, ***vieille ami***,' as he climbed into his seat. Without any direction from Pierre, the wagon would roll down St Catherine Street, turn right along Roslyn Avenue; then left on Prince Edward Street. The horse

stroked: patted lovingly
Saint Joseph: Biblical figure, married to Mary, the mother of Jesus
boast: show off
hitched: fastened
Bonjour: (French) Good day/ Good morning
vieille ami: (French) old friend

would stop at the first house, allow Pierre perhaps thirty seconds to get down from his seat and place a bottle of milk at the front door before skipping two houses and stopping at the third. Then Joseph would turn around and come back along the other side without any guidance. Pierre would boast: 'I never touch the reins. He knows just where to stop. Why, a blind man could handle my route with Joseph pulling the wagon.'

It went on for years – always the same. Pierre and Joseph both grew old together. Pierre's huge walrus moustache slowly turned pure white and Joseph didn't lift his knees so high.

Food for thought

The official language of Montreal is French because the city has a large population of French origin.

How do we know that Pierre had a remarkable memory?

Pierre appeared one morning at the stables, carrying a heavy walking stick. 'Hey, Pierre,' Jacques, the **foreman**, laughed. 'Maybe you got the **gout**, hey?'

'***Mais oui,*** Jacques,' Pierre said a bit uncertainly. 'One grows old. One's legs get tired.'

'You should teach that horse to carry the milk to the front door for you,' Jacques teased, 'he does everything else.' Joseph knew everyone of the forty families they served on Prince Edward Street.

Pierre could neither read nor write, so instead of leaving the usual note in an empty bottle if an additional quart of milk was needed, the cooks would sing out 'Bring an extra quart this morning, Pierre.'

However, Pierre had a remarkable memory. He'd always remember to tell Jacques, 'The Paquins took an extra quart this morning; the Lemoines bought a pint of cream.' Jacques would note these things in a little book he always carried. All Pierre had to do was arrive at five in the morning, walk to his wagon, which was always in the same spot at the **curb**, and deliver his milk. He returned some two hours later, got down stiffly from his seat, called a cheery '***au revoir***' to Jacques, and then limped slowly down the street.

One morning the president of the Provincale Milk Company came to inspect the early morning deliveries. Jacques pointed Pierre out to him and said: 'Watch how he talks to that horse. See how the horse listens and how he turns his head toward Pierre? I think those two share a secret. Pierre is a good man, Monsieur President, but he is old. Perhaps he could be **retired** with a small **pension**?' he added anxiously.

---

foreman: someone in charge of a group of workers

gout: painful swelling in the joints, especially of the toes

Mais oui: (French) But yes

curb: pavement, footpath

au revoir: (French) goodbye

retired: to leave a job, especially at an old age

pension: a regular payment made to a retired employee

'But of course,' the president agreed. 'I know his record. Tell him it is time he rested. His salary will go on just the same.'

But Pierre was **panic-stricken** at the thought of not driving Joseph every day. 'We are two old men,' he said to Jacques. 'Let us **wear out** together. When Joseph is ready to retire, then I, too, will **quit**.'

Jacques understood. He knew that each drew some hidden strength from the other. When Pierre and Joseph were travelling together, neither seemed old. But when they finished their work, Pierre would limp down the street slowly, and the horse's head would drop and he would walk wearily to his stall.

What did Joseph understand?

Then one chilly morning Jacques had dreadful news for Pierre when he arrived. 'Pierre, Joseph did not wake up this morning. He was twenty-five. That is like being seventy-five for a man.'

'Yes,' Pierre accepted slowly. 'I am seventy. And I cannot see Joseph again.'

'Jacques **clapped** him on the shoulder. 'We'll find another horse just as good as Joseph. We will …

He stopped. For years Pierre had worn a heavy cap which came low over his eyes. Now Jacques looked into Pierre's eyes and was startled. There was a dead, lifeless look in them. The eyes mirrored the grief in Pierre's heart and his soul[1].

Common idioms and proverbs

1. This refers to the proverb, **the eyes are the mirror to the soul**. It means that we can understand a person's thoughts by looking into their eyes. Pierre's eyes showed the grief he felt at Joseph's death.

'Take today off, Pierre,' Jacques advised, but Pierre was already **hobbling** off down the street. Tears **streamed** down his cheeks. Pierre walked to the corner and stepped into the street. There was a warning shout from the driver of a huge truck and the scream of brakes, but Pierre heard neither.

Five minutes later an ambulance driver said, 'He's dead. He was killed instantly.'

Jacques and several of the milk wagon drivers had arrived and they looked down at the still figure.

'I couldn't help it,' the driver of the truck **protested**, 'he walked right into my truck, as though he were blind.'

---

panic-stricken: too scared to think or act normally
wear out: (here) tire or become useless eventually
quit: leave
clapped: (here) slapped in a friendly manner
hobbling: walking with a limp
streamed: flowed
protested: (here) said forcefully

The ambulance doctor bent down. 'Of course the man was blind. See those **cataracts**? He has been blind for five years.'

He turned to Jacques, 'Didn't you know he was blind?'

'No... no...' Jacques said, softly. 'None of us knew. Only one knew, a friend of his named Joseph... It was a secret, I think, just between those two.'

cataracts: layers over the eyes which stop a person from seeing properly

About the author

Quentin James Reynolds (1902–1965) was an American journalist. He is described as one of the bravest World War II correspondents. Reynolds also authored books like *The Wounded Don't Cry* and *A London Diary*.

Comprehension

A. Choose the correct option.

1. Pierre Dupin's loyal companion for thirty years had been a ______________ horse named Joseph.
   a. white   b. brown   c. black
2. Every morning, ______________ would greet ______________ with the words 'Bonjour, vieille ami'.
   a. Pierre, Jacques   b. Jacques, Pierre   c. Pierre, Joseph
3. Pierre could not ______________________________.
   a. read or write.
   b. get down from the horse without help.
   c. remember things well.

B. Answer these questions in a few lines.

1. What did Pierre say about Joseph's nature when he first saw him?
2. Briefly describe the morning routine of delivering milk followed by Pierre and Joseph.
3. What was the first indication that both Pierre and Joseph were ageing together?
4. Why was Pierre panic-stricken?
5. What was the terrible news that Jacques had to give Pierre? What was the milkman's reaction to the news?

C. Answer the questions with reference to context.

1. *'You should teach that horse to carry the milk to the front door for you,' Jacques teased, 'he does everything else.'*
   a. Who was Jacques and whom was he teasing?

b. What did 'everything else' refer to with regard to the work which the horse did?

c. What had the person spoken to just said, which made Jacques say the above lines?

2. *'He walked right into my truck, as though he were blind.'*

a. Who is the speaker and who is he speaking about?

b. What did they discover about the person being referred to in the above line?

c. Who else was present at the time?

Life Skills and Values — bond between humans and animals, showing sympathy

1. In the beginning, what secret did Jacques think that Pierre and Joseph shared? What was the actual 'secret' which they shared?
2. What kind of bond did Pierre and Joseph share? Give two examples of their closeness to each other.
3. Was Jacques a good boss to Pierre? How do we know?

Vocabulary

contextual usage: action words

A. Fill in the blanks with the correct options.

1. The little boy was gently ________________ (stroking, straightening) the injured squirrel.
2. The workers ________________ (loaded, hitched) the coal onto the goods train.
3. First I shall ________________ (inspect, accept) the kitchen, then I shall check the stores.
4. The injured player ________________ (travelled, hobbled) out of the field.
5. The captain ________________ (clapped, startled) the players on the back to congratulate them for winning the game.
6. Rain water ________________ (streamed, screamed) down the hillside.

analogies

An **analogy** is a comparison between two things which share a common quality.

Examples: **Mumbai** is to **India**, what **Montreal** is to **Canada**. (relationship: large cities); **cry** is to **sadness**, what **laugh** is to **happiness** (relationship: expressing feelings)

This can also be shown as:
Mumbai : India :: Montreal : Canada
cry : sadness :: laugh : happiness

B. Look at the words in bold. Then, circle the correct option to complete the analogy.

1. **milk : cream** (*relationship: what we get from them*)
   a. cocoa : chocolate   b. cucumber : green   c. tamarind : sour
2. **stable : horse**
   a. horns : cattle   b. pen : sheep   c. honey : bees
3. **gout : bones**
   a. cough : soup   b. cataract : eyes   c. hair : brown
4. **truck : driver**
   a. boat : oars   b. aeroplane : pilot   c. sailor : sea
5. **startled : surprised**
   a. scream : loud   b. arrived : departed   c. panic : fear
6. **carriage : road**
   a. boat : water   b. glider : wings   c. cycle : ride

Grammar

types of adjectives

You know that adjectives are words that describe nouns or pronouns. There are three main kinds of adjectives.

Adjectives of quality describe the quality of a noun, such as colour, age, size and material.

Example: I will name him after the **good** Saint Joseph, who was also a **gentle** and **beautiful** spirit.

Adjectives of quantity tell us how much of something there is. They are used with countable and uncountable nouns.

Example: Each drew **some** hidden strength from the other.

Adjectives of number tell us how many people, animals or things there are.

Examples: We are **two** old men.

A. Fill in the blanks with the correct adjectives and state their type.

1. The Buddha remained ______________ but the crowd was ______________ on hearing the thunder.
   a. quiet, thunderstruck   b. calm, panic-stricken
2. Please add ______________ salt to the ______________ fish.
   a. some, fried   b. many, cold
3. The Taj Mahal is one of the ______________ examples of ______________ architecture.
   a. shortest, European   b. grandest, Mughal

4. Jupiter has ________________ moons, while the Earth has just ________________
   a. seventy-nine, one b. one, seventy-nine
5. Sid wanted to eat ________________ of the ________________ cake.
   a. half, chocolate b. full, carrot
6. Of the ________________ gifts I received on my birthday, I like the ________________ mouth organ the most.
   a. several, man-made b. many, handmade

agreement of subject and verb

When the subject of a sentence is singular, it is always accompanied by a singular verb. When the subject is plural, then the verb too must be plural. This is known as the **agreement of subject and verb**.

Examples: Pierre **walks** with a limp.
The workers **walk** in a line.

In the first sentence, the subject *Pierre* is singular. Hence, it takes the singular verb *walks*. In the second sentence, the subject *workers* is plural. Hence, it takes the plural verb *walk*.

B. Fill in the blanks with the correct options.

1. What ________________ (does/do) she like to eat?
2. I ________________ (visit/visits) my grandparents on weekends.
3. We ________________ (stand/stands) up during the national anthem.
4. The music ________________ (sound/sounds) wonderful.
5. Suniti and her friends ________________ (is/are) flying kites on the terrace.
6. Everybody ________________ (know/knows) that the Earth is round.
7. The news ________________ (is/are) read by the journalist.

Study Skills

Dictionary Skills

measurement words

We came across the words *quart* and *pint* in the story. They are units of measurement. Measurement words like *centimetre*, *kilometre*, *foot* and *litre* tell us about the size, weight, length, height and volume of things.

Look up the dictionary and write the meanings of the following measurement words.

1. gallon
2. pound
3. litre
4. yard
5. tonne
6. quart
7. ounce
8. quintal
9. pint

Listening

listening for directions

Listen to Amanda giving directions to her friend, Hannah, on how to find her house. Use a pencil to mark the route that Amanda wants her friend Hannah to take on the given map.

Then, answer the following questions.

1. What had Amanda mailed to Hannah?
2. Where will she take Hannah?
3. What does Amanda hope?

Dictation

You will now listen to a passage about a young horse and write it down. Each sentence will be repeated twice. Listen carefully and be careful not to make any spelling errors.

Speaking

expressing condolences

We offer our condolences to show our sympathy for someone's loss. Work in pairs to enact an imaginary conversation where Jacques offers his condolences to Pierre's wife about the loss of her husband. You can include the following points:

- Pierre's friendship with his horse
- Jacques' admiration for how punctual Pierre was
- how Jacques' day began as Pierre would greet him with a 'bonjour'
- how he saw master and animal grow old together

Useful words and phrases

I am very sorry for your loss ...	I always admired how ...
Please accept my sincere condolences...	We shall all miss Pierre very much ...
	If you need anything, please ...

Writing

Complete the following story.

Malti was new in town. She had not made any friends yet. She spent most of her evenings at home. It was raining hard one evening. Malti looked out of the window and saw a little girl standing under the shade of a tree...

Plan your story along the following points.

Theme: the aspect of friendship which the story highlights

Setting: where the story takes place

Characters: names and descriptions of the main characters

Plot: how the story develops. It should include an interesting event (climax).

Self-Assessment

Now I can...

- o appreciate a story about the friendship between a man and an animal.
- o contextually use action words from the story and understand analogies.
- o identify the types of adjectives and understand the agreement of subject and verb.
- o listen to directions and mark a route on a map.
- o express my condolences about someone's loss and complete a story.

Read at Leisure

Clare and her Captain: This book by Michael Morpurgo is about the friendship which develops between a young girl, an ageing horse and his lonely owner during a summer vacation in the English countryside.

Lassie Come-Home: This heart-warming story by Eric Knight is about a dog who travels many miles to be reunited with her young master.

4 Mary Makes a Friend

novel

Frances Hodgson Burnett

Reading

This extract is taken from the novel, The Secret Garden. *Mary is a ten-year-old orphan who has come to live in her wealthy uncle's house in Yorkshire, England. A spoiled and lonely girl, Mary had lived in India, where she was used to everything being done for her. In her huge new home, she is left to herself. Her uncle is often not present and the housekeeper, Mrs Medlock, does not like her. Her only companion is the young maid, Martha. Will Mary find a friend in Martha? Read on to find out.*

Mrs Medlock had allowed Martha to sleep all night in the cottage, but she was back at her work in the morning with cheeks redder than ever and in the best of spirits.

'I got up at four o'clock,' she said. 'It was pretty on the **moor** with the birds waking up and the rabbits **scampering** about and the sun rising.[1] A man gave me a ride in his cart, which I enjoyed very much.'

Martha was full of stories about her day off. Her mother had been glad to see her. They had got the baking and washing all out of the way. She had even made each of the children a doughcake with a bit of brown sugar in it.

In the evening, they had all sat round the fire, and Martha and her mother had sewn patches on torn clothes and mended **stockings**. Martha had told them about the little girl who had come from India, where everything was done for her, until she didn't know how to put on her own stockings.

'They wanted to know all about you,' said Martha, 'and the ship you came in. I couldn't tell them enough.'

'I'll tell you more before your next day off,' Mary said, 'so that you have stories to tell your brothers and sisters. They must want to hear about riding on elephants and camels, and about the officers going to hunt tigers.'

Literary term

1. This is an example of **imagery**. Martha's description of dawn on the moor creates a visual image of daily life in the English countryside.

Food for thought

India was a colony of the British Empire in the nineteenth century. Many British people travelled to India to work as soldiers and government officers. Many married and raised families there, like Mary's parents.

moor: area of open, high uncultivated land
scampering: running with quick light steps
stockings: long socks made of nylon or silk, worn by women

'My word!' cried a delighted Martha. 'It would make them **go off their heads**. Would you really do that, Miss? It would be the same as a wild beast show like we heard they had in York once.'

'India is quite different from Yorkshire,' Mary said, as she thought the matter over. 'I never thought of that. Did Dickon and your mother like hearing about me?'

'Mother asked why you were all by yourself. She said, "Hasn't Mr Craven got a **governess** for her, or a nurse?"'

What did Martha's mother ask her about Mary?

'I don't want a governess,' said Mary sharply.

'But mother says you ought to be studying at your age and you should have someone to look after you. She said, "Now, Martha, just think how you'd feel yourself, in a big place like that, wandering about all alone, and no mother. You do your best to cheer her up," she said, and I said I would.'

Mary gave her a long, steady look.

'You do cheer me up,' she said. 'I like to hear you talk.'

Then Martha went out of the room and came back with something held in her hands under her apron.

'I've brought you a present,' she said, with a cheerful grin.

'A present!' exclaimed Mary. How could a cottage full of fourteen hungry people give anyone a present, she thought.

'A man was **peddling** his **wares** across the moor,' Martha explained. 'And he stopped his cart at our door. He had pots and pans and **odds and ends**. But mother had no money to buy anything. Just as he was going away, our Elizabeth Ellen called out, "Mother, he's got skipping ropes with red and blue handles."'

What did Mary think when Martha gave her a present?

They cost two **pence** and Mother said to me, "Martha, you brought me your **wages** like a good **lass**, and I have four places to spend for every penny we have, but I'm just going to take **tuppence** out of it to buy that child a skipping rope."'

go off their heads: feel extremely excited and happy
governess: a woman hired to teach children in a private household
peddling: trying to sell small goods, while moving from place to place
wares: articles offered for sale
odds and ends: small items that are not valuable or are not part of a larger set
pence : plural for penny
wages : a fixed regular payment paid in return for work done
lass: a girl or young woman
tuppence: sum of two pennies

Martha now brought the rope out from under her apron. It was a strong, slender rope with a striped red and blue handle at each end. But Mary Lennox had never seen a skipping rope before.

'What is it for?' she asked curiously.

'You don't mean to say that you didn't have skipping ropes in India?' Martha cried out. 'This is what it's for; just watch me.'

Literary term

2. This is an example of **personification.** The portraits are imagined to be people staring at Martha, and wondering what she is doing.

She ran into the middle of the room and, taking a handle in each hand, began to skip, while Mary turned in her chair to stare at her. The **grave** faces in the old portraits seemed to stare at her too, and wonder what on earth the little girl was doing under their very noses.[2]

But Martha went on skipping without a care, until she had reached a hundred.

'I could skip longer than that,' she said, stopping. 'I've skipped as much as five hundred when I was twelve, but I wasn't out of practice then as I am now.'

Mary got up from her chair. She was beginning to feel excited herself.

'It looks nice,' she said. 'Your mother is a kind woman. Do you think I could ever skip like that?'

'Just try it,' said Martha, handing her the rope. 'You might not skip a hundred at first, but if you practise you'll go up.' Mother says, "Nothing will do her more good than a skipping rope. It's the most sensible toy a child can have. Let her play outside in the fresh air, skipping. It will stretch her legs and arms and add some strength in them."'

Mary didn't have a great deal of strength in her arms and legs. But she liked skipping so much that she did not want to stop.

Common idioms and proverbs

Practice makes perfect: This idiom tells us that with regular practice, we can all become good at a new or difficult activity.

'Put on your things and run and skip out of doors,' said Martha. 'Mother said I must tell you to keep out of doors as much as you can, even when it rains a bit. Just wrap yourself up warmly.'

Mary put on her coat and hat and took her skipping rope over her arm. She opened the door to go out, then suddenly thought of something and turned back slowly.

grave: serious

'Martha,' she said, 'they were your wages. It was your two pence, really. Thank you.'

She said it stiffly. She had not often thanked people before, far less notice when they did something for her.

'Thank you,' she said, and held out her hand because she did not know what else to do.

Martha gave her hand a clumsy little shake. She was not used to this sort of thing either. Then she laughed.

'Eh! You are a strange one,' she said. 'If it had been our Elizabeth Ellen, she would have kissed my cheek.'

Mary looked stiffer than ever.

'Should I have kissed your cheek too?'

Martha laughed again.

'Nay,' she answered. 'If you were different, perhaps you would have. But you aren't. Run off outside and play with your rope.'

Food for thought

Skipping rope as a sport may have originated in ancient Greece. It was also popular in ancient Egypt and China.

Mary felt a little **awkward** as she went out of the room. Yorkshire people seemed strange, and Martha was a puzzle to her. At first she had disliked her very much. But the skipping rope was a wonderful thing. She counted and skipped, until her cheeks were quite red, and she was more interested in the natural world around her than she had ever been.

Mary looked around. The sun was shining and a little wind was blowing. It came in delightful little **gusts** and brought a fresh scent of newly turned earth with it.

awkward: shy and ashamed, especially among people one doesn't know well
gust: strong rush of wind

About the author

Frances Hodgson Burnett (1849–1924) was a British-American playwright and author. She is well known for her novels, including *Little Lord Fauntleroy, A Little Princess* and *The Secret Garden*. She often showed working-class life in realistic detail in her books.

Comprehension

A. Compare Martha and Mary and complete the table.

	Similarities	Differences
Martha		
Mary		

B. Answer the questions in a few lines.

1. How had Martha spent her day off?
2. What did Mary plan to tell Martha before her next day off?
3. Why did Martha's mother feel that Mary should have a governess?
4. What did Martha give Mary as a present? Did she like it?
5. What did Martha advise Mary to do with the skipping rope?

C. Answer the questions with reference to context.

1. *'I don't want a governess,' said Mary sharply.*
   a. Who was Mary speaking to?
   b. Give another word for 'sharply' to describe Mary's tone.
   c. Why do you think Mary did not want a governess?
2. *'If you were different, perhaps you would have. But you aren't.'*
   a. Who said these words and to whom?
   b. What, according to the speaker, would the person spoken to have done had she been different?
   c. What had the listener actually done? What does it tell you about the person being referred to?

Life Skills and Values — appreciating kindness

1. Why did Mary call Martha's mother a kind woman?
2. Why do you think Mary disliked Martha at first?
3. Do you think Mary finally appreciated Martha? Give reasons for your answer.

Vocabulary

contextual usage

Fill in the blanks with the following phrases from the story. You may have to change the form of some words.

go off one's head	without a care	out of practice
peddling one's wares	odds and ends	stretch one's legs

1. Two hours after the flight took off, Leela got up to ________________ along the aisle.
2. As Sheena had not played the piano for years, she was quite ________________
3. David has no money, but he goes through life ________________ in the world.
4. The old woman has been ________________ in our neighbourhood for the last ten years.
5. My drawer is filled with little ________________
6. The brothers ________________ with excitement when they saw the amount of money they had won in the lottery.

Grammar

definite and indefinite articles

Read this sentence.

She had even made each of **the** children **a** doughcake and **an** apple pie.

The three articles *a*, *an* and *the* are used before nouns.

The **indefinite articles** *a* and *an* are used before singular countable nouns to refer to a person or thing in general.

The article *a* is used before a noun that begins with a consonant sound while the article *an* is used before a noun that begins with a vowel sound.

Now read this sentence.

It was pretty on **the** moor with **the** birds waking up and **the** rabbits scampering about and **the** sun rising.

The **definite article** *the* is used before a particular person or thing.

A. Fill in the blanks with the correct articles.

1. My parents gave me __________ watch for my tenth birthday.
2. __________ sun is very bright and warm today.
3. We have to buy __________ vase to replace the one we broke yesterday.
4. __________ Victorial Memorial is in Kolkata.
5. I have to buy some pencils and __________ eraser.
6. __________ nightingale sings sweet melodies.

determiners

Read these sentences.

It will stretch her legs and arms and add **some** strength in them.

It came in delightful **little** gusts.

She ran into the middle of the room and took a handle in **each** hand.

I have four places to spend for **every** penny we have.

Words like *some*, *any*, *little*, *few*, *each*, *every* are **determiners**. They give information about the quantity of countable and uncountable nouns.

B. Fill in the blanks with the correct options.

1. May I have ____________ (too/some) more milk to drink?
2. I don't want to eat ____________ (any/little) more rice.
3. There is very ____________ (few/little) time left to complete your homework.
4. We would like ____________ (all/every) student to get a prize.
5. The dancer wore bangles on ____________ (any/each) hand.
6. Very ____________ (few/less) children wanted to study for their test.

Study Skills

Pronunciation

diphthongs

A **diphthong** is a vowel sound formed by the combination of two vowels in a single syllable.

A. Say these words aloud. Notice how the two vowels in each word combine to form a single sound.

1. p**au**se   **au**thor
2. f**oo**d   bamb**oo**
3. b**oi**l   p**oi**nt
4. cl**ou**d   f**ou**nd

B. Divide the following words into four lists, according to the pronunciation of the diphthongs. Write the diphthong at the top of each column. Then, add a word of your own with the same diphthong.

hoist	fault	ouch	shampoo	round	oil
room	join	tool	pauper	loud	vault

au			ou
	oil		

Listening

listening for details

Listen to a poem on friendship and answer the questions.

1. What do we do when our spirits need a lift?
2. Why do we treasure a friend?
3. What do we laugh about with our friends?
4. When do we become serious with a friend?
5. What does a friend fill our life with?
6. How does a friend change the world we live in?

Speaking

conversation: offering advice

Work in pairs. Imagine that you and your partner are Martha and Mary. You want to advise Mary to spend more time outdoors playing. Enact the conversation.

You may begin in this way.

Martha: Miss Mary, you should go outdoors more often.

Mary: It's cold and windy outside. I want to stay at home.

Martha: Why don't you take your skipping rope?

Useful words and phrases

- *You should go* out and explore.
- *Why don't you* go out and play?
- *You ought to* get more exercise.
- *You could go* to the local market.
- *If I were you, I would* never stay indoors all day.
- *I would advise* returning home before it is dark.

Writing

Imagine you are Mary. Write a diary entry narrating what happened the day Martha gave you a skipping rope. You can include the following points in your entry.

- how excited Martha was after returning from her day off
- your surprise at receiving an unexpected gift
- how you felt about thanking Martha for the gift
- your experience of skipping for the first time
- what you learnt from the events of that day

Self-Assessment

Now I can...

- o read and appreciate a story about kindness and friendship.
- o understand and use idomatic phrases from the story.
- o use articles and determiners correctly.
- o pronounce words with diphthongs and offer advice to someone.
- o write a diary entry.

Read at Leisure

Anne of Green Gables: This book by L. M. Montgomery is about the adventures of Anne Shirley, an eleven-year-old orphan who uses her imagination and determination to win against all odds in life.

The BFG: This book by Roald Dahl is about the unexpected friendship between Sophie, an orphan girl and a soft-hearted giant, who is very different from the cruel giants among whom he lives.

III

Peace and Harmony

Take Off

A. Identify the Nobel Peace Prize winners with the help of the given clues.

Malala Yousafzai   Kofi Annan   the Dalai Lama
Barack Obama   Nelson Mandela

1. This spiritual leader spread the message of peace and non-violent opposition against the occupation of Tibet ____________
2. He was a South African leader who helped end Apartheid, or the policy of discrimination against non-white people. He spent 27 years in prison for his struggle. ____________

3. This Pakistani girl raised her voice against the suppression of young people and for the right of all children to education. She was shot at by a Taliban gunman but survived. ____________
4. He was the first African American President of the USA, who made efforts to increase cooperation between the people of the world. ____________
5. He was the Secretary-General of the United Nations from 1997 to 2006. He was from Ghana, Africa. ____________

B. Can you recognize these tribes from various parts of the world? Write their names by filling in the missing letters using the clues.

1. M_SA_ (nomadic herder tribe from Kenya and Tanzania in Africa)

2. A _ _ C H _ (tribe of fierce warriors, who lived in America)

3. I _ U _ T (group of tribes from Canada, Greenland and Alaska. They live in igloos in winter.)

Answers are given at the end of the chapter.

5 When the Twins Went to War

Aaron Shepard

Reading

Do you fight with your friends when you want something or to prove that you are right? How do you feel when the fight is resolved? Read this humorous play, based on a Russian fable, to find out how two warring tribes laid down arms.

Characters

Narrator 1 **Narrator 2**
Chubak and Udoga, ***the wise twins***
Beldy chief and his wife
Beldy hunter
Other Beldy men and women
Zaksuli chief and his wife
Zaksuli women

> **Literary term**
>
> 1. and 2. These two lines are examples of **repetition**. The same words or phrases are repeated to create a musical effect and emphasize the love for war the Beldy people had.

Narrator 1: In Far East Russia, the Amur river area was home to many **native** tribes who lived for centuries by hunting and fishing. In the **tribe** of the Nanai, the ones who most loved to fight were the men of the Beldy **clan**.

Narrator 2: They were always rushing off to attack another clan's village, or defending themselves from a clan that had come for revenge.

Narrator 1: They **neglected** their hunting.[1]

Narrator 2: They neglected their fishing.[2]

Narrator 1: They were so dedicated to it that they felt lost when they weren't fighting. They just sat around and waited for the next war.

Narrator 2: Every year, there were fewer of them left alive.

Narrator 1: Into this clan was born a pair of twins whose names were ...

Chubak: Chubak

native: belonging to a region or country by birth
tribe: a group of people of the same race, language, and customs
clan: a group which consists of families that are related to each other
neglected: failed to take care of

Narrator 1: and ...

Udoga: Udoga

Narrator 2: The Beldies were careful to honour the boys because they believed that twins brought good luck.

Why did the Beldies honour the boys?

Narrator 1: Besides, there was something special about those two. By the time they were five years old, they were wiser than anyone else in the village.

Narrator 2: Both the men and women of the clan often came to them for advice.

Narrator 1: One day, a Beldy hunter found that one of his traps had been sprung, but the animal was missing.

Narrator 2: He could tell from the signs that the animal was a **weasel** and that it had been taken by a man of the Zaksuli clan.

Hunter *(indignantly to himself)*: A Zaksuli stole my weasel!

Narrator 1: The hunter went to tell the Beldy chief.

Beldy chief *(angrily)*: This is a great **insult**! *(to the Beldy men)* Prepare for war!

Beldy men and the hunter *(shouting all at once)*: A war! A war!

Narrator 1: All the Beldy men rushed off eagerly to get their spears, knives, bows and arrows ready.

Beldy chief's wife: Not again! Is a weasel worth killing and dying for?

Beldy chief: We are men. Must a man not fight?

Beldy chief's wife: You are men! Must a man be stupid?

Narrator 1: She went with the other Beldy women to talk with the twins.

Beldy chief's wife: Udoga, Chubak, tell the men to stay home. We have had enough fighting and killing.

Beldy women *(speaking all at once)*: That's right. We have had enough. Tell them to stay home.

Chubak *(to Udoga)*: She's right, brother. There has been enough war.

Udoga: We'll see what we can do.

Narrator 2: Not long after, the men also came to the twins.

weasel: a small wild animal with reddish-brown fur, a long thin body and short legs

indignantly: in an angry or surprised way because of something unfair that has happened

insult: a remark or an action that is said or done to offend somebody

Beldy chief: Chubak, Udoga, give us your **counsel**.

Chubak *(picking up a warrior's bow)***:** Never has a clan been so insulted! If the thief had taken a **sable**, we could forgive him. The skin of a sable has value. But a weasel skin is almost worthless. It must have been taken just to shame us. If we are shamed, we have no honour. If we have no honour, we are dead. The Zaksulis have killed us!

Beldy men and chief *(excitedly)***:** That's right! That's right!

Udoga *(picking up a spear)***:** We must go back and defeat the Zaksulis! But wait! The Zaksulis are our enemies. So, we must take a **vow** not to eat any food from their land or drink a single drop of their water.

Beldy men and chief *(together)***:** We swear it! We swear it! Defeat the Zaksulis! Zaksulis, here we come!

Narrator 1: The women were sad.

Beldy chief's wife: What hope do we have, when even the twins go to war?

Food for thought

Throughout history, people have tried many ways to avoid war. One of these is sport, which has been used since ancient times to solve disagreements peacefully. For example, the Olympic Games were started as a 'replacement' for war, in which tribes tried to beat each other through their representatives.

What vows did Udoga make the Beldy warriors take?

Narrator 2: They set about preparing the men's food.

Narrator 1: The next morning, the men loaded themselves with as much food and water as they could carry.

Narrator 2: Then, taking the twins with them, they started off towards the Zaksuli village.

Narrator 1: They walked all day. It was slow, hard going, with all they had to carry. The farther they went, the angrier they were at the Zaksulis.

Beldy men and chief *(together, loudly)*: Just wait till we meet the Zaksulis in battle! They will never dare to take on the Beldies again!

Narrator 2: They came upon some Zaksuli women gathering berries.

Chubak *(angrily)*: Hear, O women, we are coming to your village! We will defeat you all! Generations will remember the fight between the Beldies and the Zaksulis.

Zaksuli women *(to each other)*: Oh no! The Beldies! It's the Beldies!

counsel: advice
sable: (here) a small furry animal, valued for its fur
vow: a serious promise or decision to do a particular thing

Narrator 2: The women ran off to warn their men.

Beldy chief *(in dismay, to Chubak)*: Why did you let them know? With all that we are carrying, those women will reach the village long before we do. The men will hide in the lodges deep inside their village, and we'll have to wait them out!

Udoga *(To all the men)*: What is that to us? Nothing they do can save them. Death to the Zaksulis!

Beldy Men *(except the chief)*: Death to the Zaksulis! Death to the Zaksulis!

Narrator 1: The Beldies reached the village, but the Zaksuli men were already hiding inside.

Narrator 2: They were not like the Beldies. They did not want to fight. They wanted to stay put till the **warmongering** Beldies went home!

Narrator 1: The Beldies hid all around the village in the tall grass and the bushes.

Narrator 2: They knew that sooner or later the Zaksuli men would have to come out. They would need to hunt and fish. Then they would have to face the Beldies.

Narrator 1: The next morning, the Zaksuli men did not come out.

Narrator 2: But the women came out. They carried big sticks.

Zaksuli chief's wife: You foolish Beldies! Why don't you go back to your village where you belong?

Narrator 2: The women found the Beldies hiding in the grass and the bushes. They began beating them with their sticks.

Who beat up the Beldy warriors with sticks?

Zaksuli women and chief's wife: Take that, you silly men! Go home!

Beldy men and chief: Ow! Ow! Ow!

Udoga *(to the men)*: Be brave! Remember, you must never hit a woman!

Beldy chief: But what if the woman hurts us?—Ow!

Chubak: How does that matter? We are men. How could a woman hurt us?

Narrator 1: Soon all the Beldy men were getting a sound beating from the Zaksuli women.

Beldy men and chief: Ow! Ow! Ow!

Narrator 1: Day after day, the Beldies waited for the Zaksuli men.

Narrator 2: Every day, the women came out and beat them.

Beldy men and chief (*suffering another beating*): Ow! Ow!

warmongering: wanting to start a war or encouraging people to start a war

Narrator 1: The Beldy men were brave.

Narrator 2: Then their food ran out.

Chubak: Remember your vow! We will take no food from this evil land![3]

Beldy chief: But how can we fight without food?

Chubak: Don't worry! It won't be long now!

Beldy men and chief (*as they are beaten by the women again*): Ow! Ow!

Narrator 1: So they were brave a little longer.

Narrator 2: Then their water ran out.

Udoga: Remember your vow! Not a drop of water from this place of evil![4]

Beldy chief: But we can't last long without water.

Udoga: We won't have to. We've almost won!

Narrator 2: But their patience ran out.

Beldy chief: What kind of war is this? We are so weak from hunger and thirst that we can barely hold our spears!

Chubak: We are men. When honour is **at stake**, how can we complain of **hardship?**

Narrator 1: But they could not hold out anymore. They were ready to give up.

Narrator 2: At last the Zaksuli chief appeared to speak with the Beldy chief.

Zaksuli chief: Are you now ready to talk and settle this matter without fighting?

Udoga: How can talk **restore** honour? We will be satisfied only by a great gift.

Chubak: Yes, a gift such as never given before.

Zaksuli chief *(trembling)*: What do you want?

Udoga: You must give us ... (*pausing for effect*) ... the skin of the weasel!

Narrator 2: Both the chiefs stared at the twins in astonishment. Then the Zaksuli chief ran back to tell the good news.

Narrator 1: The Beldy chief's face grew red.

Beldy chief: Is that such a worthy gift? Is that why we starved and suffered? For nothing but the skin of a weasel?

Chubak *(innocently)*: The weasel skin sent us to war. Why shouldn't it send us home?

Narrator 1: The Beldy chief could not disagree with this reasoning.

Narrator 2: Back in their village, the Beldy chief spoke with his wife.

Literary term

3. and 4. The play has several **exclamations** such as these. They express strong emotions such as pride, courage and anger.

at stake: at risk
hardship: a difficult situation
restore: (here) bring back to its earlier state

Beldy chief: What a war that was! The most terrible war of all! We never want to go to war again!

Narrator 1: That was indeed the last war between the Beldies and the Zaksulis. Thanks to the twins' clever move, the Beldies learnt that fighting was of no use to anyone and war brought only suffering. They made peace with the Zaksulis. The **sworn enemies** turned into peaceful neighbours.

sworn enemies: people or countries that have a strong dislike for each other

Comprehension

A. Fill in the blanks with words from the play.

1. In the tribe of the __________, the Beldy clan loved to fight.
2. By the time they were __________ years old, the twins were wiser than anyone else in the village.
3. A Beldy hunter found that his __________ had been stolen.
4. The Beldies took a __________ to not accept food or water from the Zaksulis.
5. The Beldy men came upon some women gathering __________.
6. The __________ women beat up the Beldy warriors with __________.
7. According to Chubak, when __________ was at stake, men should not complain about __________.

B. Read the lines and answer the questions.

1. *'This is a great insult! Prepare for war!'*
   a. Who said these lines and to whom?
   b. What was the great insult?
   c. Whom did they go to for advice? What advice did they receive?
2. *'Hear, O women, we are coming to your village!'*
   a. Who said this line?
   b. Who were the women?
   c. Who is being referred to as 'we' and why had they come to the village?
3. *Both the chiefs stared at the twins in astonishment.*
   a. Who were the twins?
   b. Who were the chiefs and why were they astonished?
   c. What did the twins say to astonish them?

Life Skills and Values

non-violence, cleverness

1. Why did the Beldy women not want any more wars?
2. Why do you think the twins asked only for a weasel's skin as a gift from the Zaksulis?
3. Did Chubak really believe that a woman's beating could not hurt the Beldies?
4. Explain the clever move of the twins to stop their clan from waging wars.

Vocabulary

antonyms

A. Complete the crossword with the antonyms of the given words.

Across

3. revenge
5. defeat
7. luck
8. alive

Down

1. insult
2. neglect
4. special
6. won

Grammar

adjectives: degrees of comparison

Adjectives change form when we use them to compare two nouns or pronouns.

Read these sentences.

The Beldies were a **brave** clan. (positive degree)

The Beldies were **braver** than the Zaksuli clan. (comparative degree)

The Beldies were the **bravest** clan of all. (superlative degree)

Notice the forms the adjective *brave* takes in the positive, comparative and superlative degrees.

When we use an adjective in the **positive degree**, we do not make a comparison.

The **comparative degree** of an adjective compares two nouns or pronouns. We add *-er* after the adjective. For some adjectives, we also add *more* before the word to form the comparative degree.

Example: The story is **more suitable** for children than adults.

The **superlative degree** of an adjective compares more than two nouns or pronouns. We add *-est* after the adjective. For some adjectives, we use *most* before the word.

Example: This is the **most beautiful** painting in the gallery.

A. Rewrite the sentences after correcting the errors in the degrees of comparison.

1. Diamond is the harder substance found on Earth.
2. The apples in the orchard were fresh and juicier.
3. This film is interesting than the one we watched last week.
4. Sneha has the better handwriting in the class.
5. Sachin Tendulkar is one of the more famous cricketers in the world.
6. This math problem is simple than the last one.

interjections

Look at this line from the play.

Beldy men and chief *(suffering a beating)*: **Ow! Ow!**

The word *Ow!* expresses pain. Such words are called **interjections**. They are used to express pain, surprise, happiness and anger.

B. Fill in the blanks with the given interjections.

Hurrah! Ouch! Alas! Phew! Shh! Brr!

1. __________ I finally found the book I had been looking for.
2. __________ I hurt my knee on the edge of the table.
3. __________ The wise old man is no more.
4. __________ It is so cold today.
5. __________ Maintain silence in the library.
6. __________ We are going on a picnic.

Study Skills

Spelling

error correction

Circle the misspelled word in these sentences and write their correct spelling.

1. The criminal was plotting to take revaunge on the policeman.
2. Mr Sampath is a man of great pacience. He never loses his temper with anyone.
3. The neighbours complaned about the dog's constant barking.
4. My sister was embarassed to be caught having a midnight snack in secret.
5. It was an honner to meet my favourite author at the book fair.
6. The wise woman's councel helped the villagers solve their problems.

Listening

listening for information

Listen to a story about Akbar and Birbal and state whether the following statements are true (T) or false (F).

1. The neighbours shared their garden. ☐
2. The neighbours signed an agreement for the sale of the house. ☐
3. The farmer sold the well. ☐
4. Iqbal took water from the well. ☐
5. Birbal told the farmer to pay rent. ☐
6. The two neighbours became friends again. ☐

Speaking

conversation: expressing regret and hope

We express regret when we are sorry about something or when we wish that something did not happen.

Work in pairs. Imagine that you and your partner are two Beldy women. Enact a conversation about the foolishness of the Beldy men who want to keep fighting. One woman believes that it is a mistake to fight with one's neighbours, while the other hopes for a solution to the problem.

You may begin like this:

Woman 1: I do not understand why our men have to fight wars. We have lost so many lives.

Woman 2: Do not be so disheartened. Let us go to the twins with the chief's wife.

Useful words and phrases

Regret	Hope
• I wish...	• We/they should have...
• I hope...	• I would like...
• If only...	• May it happen...

Writing

writing an essay

Do you think there is too much violence in this world? What do you think you can do to bring about peace? Write an essay on the topic. You can use the following points in your essay:

- meaning of peace and why it is important
- examples of situations where people have suffered because of lack of peace
- how you and your friends, as young people, can teach others about the importance of non-violence

Self-Assessment

Now I can...

- o read and appreciate a play about how peace wins over war.
- o solve a crossword on antonyms.
- o use degrees of comparison of adjectives and interjections.
- o spell words from the play correctly.
- o express regret and hope, and write an essay on peace.

Read at Leisure

One Peace: True Stories of Young Activists: This book by Janet Wilson celebrates the achievements of children around the globe who have worked to promote world peace.

The Diary of a Young Girl: This book includes the diary entries of Anne Frank, a Jewish girl who hid in an attic with her family during World War II.

Answers to ***Take Off*** Exercise B

1. Masai   2. Apache   3. Inuit

lyric poem

6 Call for Peace

H. W. Longfellow

Reading

What do you think of war? What happens when people and nations fight with each other? 'The Song of Hiawatha' is an epic poem based on Native American mythology. It describes the legend of an American Indian Chief of the Onondaga tribe, called Hiawatha. This extract from the poem speaks of Gitche Manito, the Supreme Being, who created all and filled everything with life force. He comes down from the skies and tells the warring tribes of the Earth to stop fighting and live peacefully. Read this extract to find out how he tries to persuade people to live in harmony.

Gitche Manito, the mighty,
The creator of the nations,
Looked upon them with **compassion**,
With **paternal** love and pity;
Looked upon their **rage** and **wrangling**
But as quarrels among children,
But as **feuds** and fights of children![1]
Over them he stretched his right hand,
To calm their **stubborn** natures,
To cool their thirst and **fever**,
By the shadow of his right hand;
Spake to them with voice majestic
As the sound of far-off waters,
Falling into deep **abysses**,
Warning, **chiding,** spake in these words:—

Food for thought

Long before Europeans colonized the Americas, it was inhabited by various Native American tribes. Hiawatha, the legendary chief, is known for bringing together five warring tribal nations. He also called for peace with the European settlers.

Literary term

1. This is a **simile**. The warring people are compared to quarelling children.

compassion: a feeling of pity, sympathy and understanding
paternal: fatherly
rage: strong anger that is difficult to control
wrangling: long argument
feuds: long bitter quarrels
stubborn: unwilling to change one's mind or behaviour
fever: (here) extreme nervous disturbance or worry
Spake: past tense of 'speak' (old English)
abysses: deep bottomless holes in the ground
chiding: scolding

'O my children! my poor children!
Listen to the words of wisdom,
Listen to the words of warning,
From the lips of the Great Spirit,
From the Master of Life, who made you!
'I have given you lands to hunt in,
I have given you streams to fish in,
I have given you bear and bison,
I have given you **roe** and reindeer,
I have given you **brant** and **beaver**,[2]
Filled the **marshes** full of wild-fowl,
Filled the rivers full of fishes;
Why then are you not **contented**?
Why then will you hunt each other?

'I am **weary** of your quarrels,
Weary of your wars and **bloodshed**,
Weary of your prayers for **vengeance**,
Of your wranglings and disagreements;
All your strength is in your union,
All your danger is in **discord**;
Therefore be at peace henceforward,
And as brothers live together.

Common idioms and proverbs

United we stand, divided we fall: This proverb is similar to Gitche Manito's words that people are strong when they work together, but they will be in danger if they keep fighting.

roe: fish eggs
brant: North American term for a small goose
beaver: a furry animal with a big flat tail
marshes: areas of low-lying lands which are full of still waters
contented: happy and satisfied
weary: very tired
bloodshed: the killing or wounding of a lot of people
vengeance: revenge taken for an injury or wrong
discord: disagreement and argument between people

About the poet

Henry Wadsworth Longfellow (1807–1882) was an American poet. He was a professor at Harvard College in the USA. His most well-known works are *The Song of Hiawatha* and *Evangeline*.

Understanding the poem

A. Choose the correct option to complete each statement.

1. Gitche Manito stretched his ________________ over the warring tribes.
   a. right hand   b. left hand   c. head
2. His voice was as powerful as ________________.
   a. far-off waters falling into deep abysses   b. quarrel among children
   c. bear and bison
3. Gitche Manito was not the ________________.
   a. Great Spirit   b. Master of Life   c. King of the Land
4. He had filled the marshes with ________________.
   a. fish   b. wild fowl   c. roe and reindeer
5. The tribes were not ________________.
   a. content   b. quarrelling   c. wrangling

B. Answer the questions with reference to context.

1. *Looked upon them with compassion/With paternal love and pity;*
   a. Who looked upon whom with compassion and pity?
   b. Why did he feel compassion and pity?
   c. Why does he look at them with paternal love?
2. *'Why then are you not contented?/Why then will you hunt each other?'*
   a. Why are the tribes not contented?
   b. Why are they hunting each other?
   c. Which figure of speech does the poet use in these lines? What effect does it create?

Life Skills and Values — importance of peace and harmony

1. Why are Gitche Manito's words of wisdom also words of warning?
2. What advice does he give his children?

Vocabulary

phrases with 'peace'

A. Look up the meanings of the phrases given in the box in a dictionary. Then fill in the blanks with the correct phrases.

keep the peace	at peace	make peace
peace offering	peace of mind	disturbing the peace

1. Matthew is ________________ with the world ever since he gave up fighting.

2. Sheela got an ice cream for her sulking brother as a ____________________
3. The police told the crowd to ____________________ and listen to them calmly.
4. Shake hands, teams, and ____________________
5. The old lady installed a new burglar alarm system to get some ____________________
6. The rowdy boys were asked to leave the concert because they were ____________________

imagery

Read these lines from the poem.
With paternal love and pity;
Looked upon their rage and wrangling
But as quarrels among children

These lines create a picture in our mind of Gitche Manito as the father and the tribes as quarrelling children. It is an example of **imagery**.

B. Describe in your own words the imagery in these lines from the poem.

1. By the shadow of his right hand
2. As the sound of far-off waters/Falling into deep abysses
3. I have given you lands to hunt in/I have given you streams to fish in…
4. Filled the marshes full of wild-fowl/Filled the rivers full of fishes

Activity

making an origami figure

A. The dove is a symbol of peace. Follow the steps given and make an origami peace dove. Write words and draw pictures of peace on your peace dove.

Materials needed:

- square sheets of paper of about 3 × 3 inches
- scissors
- pens
- markers
- paint

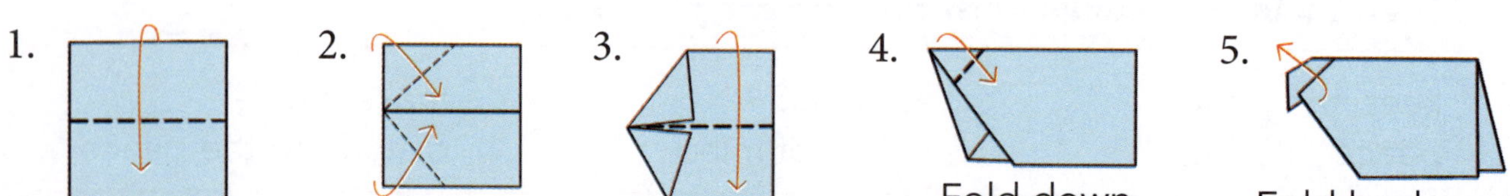

1. Fold. Unfold.
2. Fold to centre line.
3. Fold in half.
4. Fold down one-fourth of the top edge.
5. Fold back up to make the neck.

6. 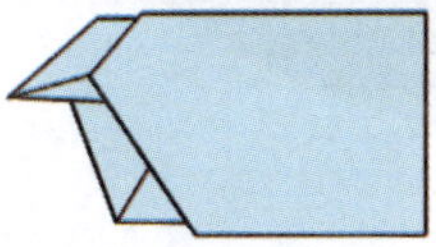

Fold back down to make the head.

7. 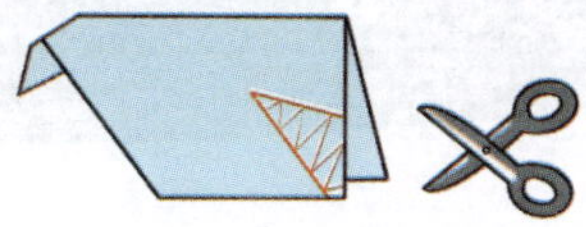

Cut to make the wings and tail.

8. 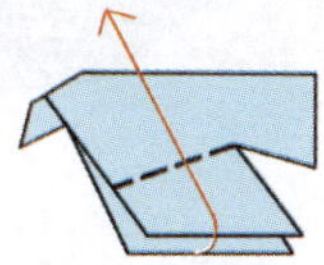

Fold wings upwards.

9. 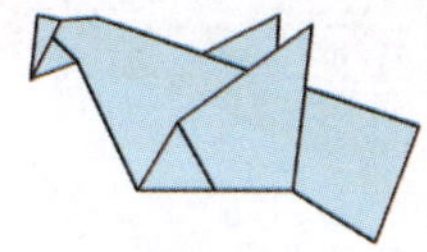

Your finished dove!

picture composition

B. Look at the pictures. What do they depict? Using them as clues, write a short paragraph contrasting war and peace.

Now I can...   **Self-Assessment**

- o read and understand a lyric poem about Native Americans.
- o use phrases with 'peace' and explain imagery.
- o make an origami peace dove and write a peace message.
- o write a paragraph based on a given picture.

Read at Leisure

A Cherokee Prayer: This moving Native Indian poem by Spiritwind Wood is a prayer in which a weary warrior prays to the Great Spirit to guide him through bloodshed and pain.

The Rainy Day: This lyric poem by H. W. Longfellow compares the sadness in the poet's heart to a rainy day.

Project 1

A. You have read how imagination and fantasy affect Jatin in 'Jatin's Sandals' and Johnny in 'Johnny Head-in-Air'. Now write a short story using your imagination and fantasy.

Ensure that the story has the following elements:

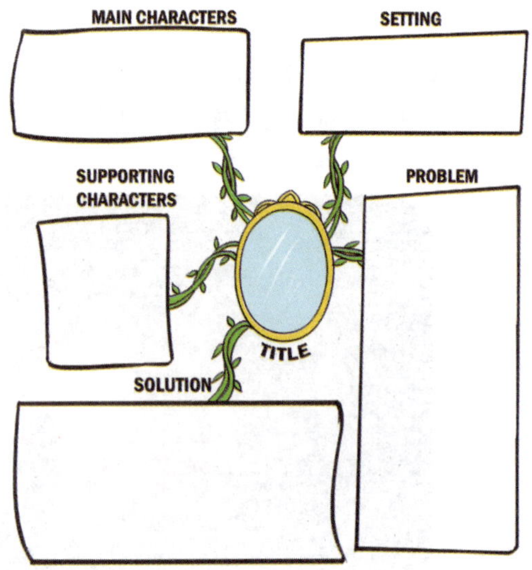

Characters: You could have one central character, a few main characters and other supporting characters. Your characters could be any of these.

- strange animals or human beings with special powers
- special machines or robots
- elves, giants, dragons or other mythical creatures

Setting: Where and when the story takes place.

Plot: This is the storyline. Make sure your plot has a beginning, a middle and an end.

Problem: This is what motivates the characters to act. This should be well-thought out, as it will make your story different from the rest.

Resolution: How the problem is solved.

Use the given story map to jot down your ideas. Put your ideas together and start writing.

Lastly, give your story an interesting **title**.

B. You have learnt about the importance of peace and harmony in the chapters 'When the Twins Went to War' and 'Call for Peace'. Many countries around the world have created symbols to promote peace. Look at some of these symbols. Find out more about them. Choose your favourite symbol and talk about it in class.

Include the following points in your talk:

- the country or culture of origin
- the story behind the origin of the sign
- if an artist had designed it, name of artist/designer and the year of design
- why you chose to talk about that particular sign

 The olive branch	 The dove	 The crane
 The white poppy	 The V symbol	 The peace sign

Now design your own peace sign and give a brief explanation of the idea behind the design.

IV

Nature and Conservation

Take Off

A. Rearrange the jumbled letters to form words related to nature and conservation.

a. SCEPEIS ___ ___ E ___ I ___ S

b. MENVRIOENNT ___ N ___ ___ R ___ ___ ___ E ___ T

c. HATABTI ___ ___ B ___ T ___ ___

d. ETCNITX ___ ___ T ___ ___ C ___

e. DEOFRESTANIOT ___ E ___ ___ R ___ S ___ AT ___ ___ N

B. Endangered animals are those that are at risk of dying out. Some species of rhinoceros are endangered today. Complete the facts about this gentle giant using the given words.

two	grass	rainforests	mud	Oxpeckers	one	herbivore
sun	plants	swamps	cries	grassy plains	insects	danger

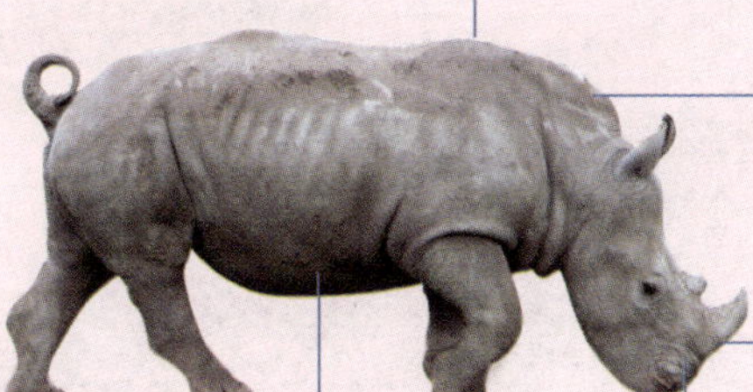

Diet: It is a ___________. It mostly feeds on ___________ and ___________.

Habitat: It is found in ___________ ___________, ___________ and ___________.

Horns: Javan and Indian rhinos have ___________ horn, while the white, black and Sumatran rhinos have ___________ horns.

Interesting facts: They like taking ___________ baths. It protects their skin from the strong ___________ and keeps off bugs.

Friend: ___________ or tick birds perch on a rhino's back, eating the ___________ living in the rhino's thick skin. The birds' loud ___________ also alert the rhino to ___________.

non-fiction

7 Sudan: The End of a Species

Reading

Faced with the loss of habitat and hunting, many wild animals have been quietly disappearing from the face of the Earth. Conservationists continue to fight to save them. Read on to find out about one such effort to save an endangered species of rhinoceros and what went wrong in the attempt.

The date of 19 March 2018 was a sad day for wildlife lovers across the world. On this day, Sudan, the world's last male northern white rhino **breathed his last**. He was 45 years old, equivalent to 90 in human years. Though he left behind a daughter and a granddaughter, his death meant the end of an entire species of rhinoceros. No new northern white rhino will ever **walk the earth** again.

Do you know how many types of rhinoceros there are in the world? There are five different **species**. These are the black rhinoceros and the white rhinoceros from Africa, and the Indian rhinoceros, the Javan rhinoceros and the Sumatran rhinoceros from South Asia.

What are the five types of rhinos in the world?

Sudan, though a 'white' rhino, was not white in colour, but grey. How do you think the white rhino got its name? It did not, in fact, refer to their colour at all. It comes from '*wijde*', the Dutch word for 'wide', which refers to their wide mouths. White rhinos have two sub-species—the northern and the southern.

Sudan, the last male northern white rhino

Sudan's story

Sudan died of age-related **complications** at the Ol Pejeta Conservancy in Kenya, Africa, where he had lived since 2009. Sudan's daughter Najin and Najin's daughter, Fatu continue to live here.

Where had Sudan lived since 2009?

breathed his last: died
walk the earth: live

species: a group of plants or animals that have the same main characteristics and can produce children

complications: (here) medical problems that occur as a result of another illness or old age

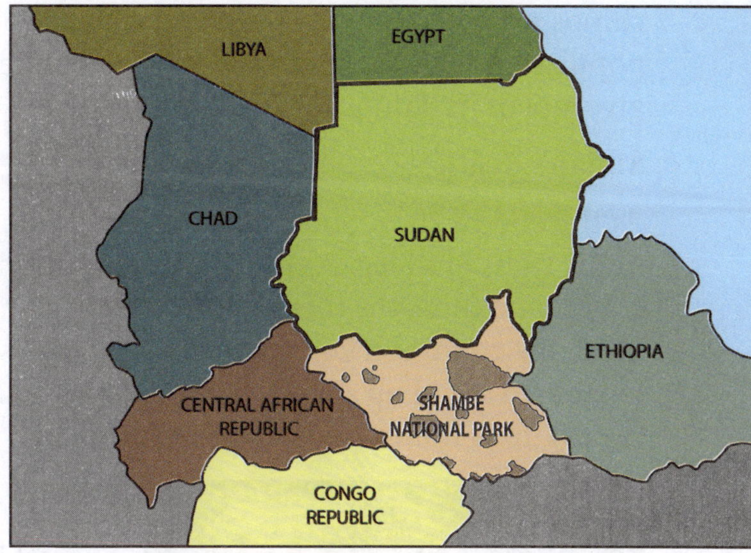

Sudan was born in 1972 in southern Sudan, Africa. He lived earlier at the Dvůr Králové Zoo in Czechoslovakia, before he was transferred to the Conservancy. The three-year-old Sudan, along with five other rhinos were captured by animal trappers and brought to the Czech zoo in 1975. Many **environmentalists** were against it at the time. They felt that the already rare animals should have been left in the wild.

Trouble in wilderness

By the 1960s, the numbers of northern white rhinos were going down across the world, mainly because of widespread **poaching**. At one time, they may have ranged over much of North Africa; but in the sixties, they had become limited to South Sudan, Uganda and two other countries. In 1969, Uganda had about 80 rhinos, but by 1982, they had all been wiped out. In 1981, **aerial surveys** were done to find more rhinos in the Shambe region, where Sudan had been captured six years ago. Only skeletal remains of seven rhinos were seen, whereas almost 200 to 300 had been alive even a year before.

By the early 2000s, the last few dozen wild northern white rhinos in the Democratic Republic of Congo had been killed. By 2008, the northern white rhino was believed to be extinct in the wild.

Why are rhinos so **prized** by poachers? It is for their horn, which contains **keratin**, the same substance that is present in our hair and nails. But **superstition** and traditional medicine have led people to believe that the horns can cure incurable diseases. Owning a rhino horn is also thought to be a **status symbol**. The horns are sold at very high prices, which increases the greed of merciless poachers. Even though Ol Pejeta has round-the-clock security, with armed guards watching over each rhino, the fear of poachers is high.

Why are rhino horns sold at very high prices?

Efforts at captive breeding

As the northern white rhinos became more endangered, the Dvůr Králové Zoo sent three of its six rhinos to the San Diego Zoo in the USA for **captive breeding**. But they died without producing any **offspring**. The remaining

environmentalists: people who work to protect the natural world
poaching: illegal hunting of animals
aerial surveys: surveys carried out from the sky, using an aeroplane or helicopter
prized: highly valued

keratin: a protein that forms hair, feathers, horns and hoofs
superstition: belief in things that are not real or possible, like magic
status symbol: something that a person owns that shows they have money and importance in society

captive breeding: keeping endangered wild animals, often in a zoo, to produce young ones
offspring: children

rhinos were now 20 years old and didn't reproduce. An attempt to set up a second wild population in Africa in 1995 failed as neither zoo would give any of its rhinos for breeding.

Common idioms and proverbs

1. **put to sleep:** This idiom refers to a situation in which a vet uses a painless method to end the life of an animal who has lost all hope of getting better.
2. **closed the door (on something):** the end of the possibility of something happening

Sudan's death

At the end of 2017, Sudan was suffering from an infection in his right hind leg. Although his condition improved after some time, the infection returned. In March 2018, his condition got worse despite **intensive care**. Unable to stand up and suffering a great deal in his last twenty-four hours, Sudan was put to sleep[1].

Southern white rhinos

White rhino conservation

At least 20,000 southern white rhinos roam southern Africa today. But the situation of northern white rhinos is **dire**. There is a small chance that a few of them might be **holed up** in a **remote** part of Africa. Many of these areas are war zones and no one has visited them for many years. Sudan's death closed the doors[2] on any possibility of natural breeding. Some experts feel that the future of the northern white rhino depends on them breeding with southern white rhinos.

Raising awareness

Sudan was a great **ambassador** for his species. In February 2015, Ol Pejeta Conservancy launched a **campaign** to raise funds for the rangers guarding the rhinos. In May 2015, there was a global campaign to help generate funds for artificial methods of breeding. Even though he is gone, Sudan's **genetic material** has been stored. This may be a ray of hope for bringing back northern white rhinos. It is said that the greatest tragedy that our world can suffer is to watch a species disappear. 'Sudan's death is **symbolic**,' says Elodie Sampere, who works at Ol Pejeta. 'If we allow the second largest mammal on the planet to go extinct, what chances do smaller species have? We are currently facing extinction at a faster rate than any other time in human history. We must use Sudan's death as a **wake-up call** for the rest of the species.'

intensive care: special care given to people or animals who are very ill or badly injured

dire: serious

holed up: staying hidden somewhere, to avoid being found

remote: faraway

ambassador: (here) representative of a species

campaign: planned set of activities carried out over a period of time to bring about change

genetic material: material that stores information about a living thing's various qualities and physical features

symbolic: (here) important because it marks a big change

wake-up call: an event that makes people realize that something serious is happening

Comprehension

A. Read the sentences. Put a cross (X) for the statement that is not true.

1. a. Sudan, the world's last male northern white rhino, was born in 1972. ☐
   b. Sudan developed an infection in his eyes in 2017. ☐
   c. Sudan died on 19 March, 2018. ☐
2. a. In 1969, Uganda had about 80 rhinos. ☐
   b. By the early eighties, the northern white rhino was almost extinct in Uganda. ☐
   c. In 1981, aerial surveys of the area where Sudan had been captured showed that there were almost 200 more rhinos. ☐
3. a. The southern white rhino is also an endangered species. ☐
   b. At least 20,000 southern white rhinos roam southern Africa. ☐
   c. Some experts feel that the future of northern white rhinos depends on breeding them with southern white rhinos. ☐
4. a. In February 2015, the Ol Pejeta Conservancy started a campaign to raise funds for artificial breeding. ☐
   b. Ol Pejeta has round-the-clock security for the rhinos. ☐
   c. Elodie Sampere says that Sudan's death is symbolic. ☐

B. Answer these questions.

1. How did the white rhino get its name even though it was grey in colour?
2. What role did the Ol Pejeta Conservancy play in the life of Sudan?
3. Why are rhinos so prized by poachers?
4. What were the results of earlier efforts at captive breeding the northern white rhinos, involving the Dvůr Králové Zoo and the San Diego Zoo?
5. How did Sudan die?
6. Why can't people search for northern white rhinos in the remote parts of Africa?
7. What is the last ray of hope for the northern white rhino?

C. Answer the questions with reference to context.

Many environmentalists were against it at the time.

a. What is being referred to as 'it' here?
b. Which year is being referred to by the word 'time'?
c. Why were the environmentalists against 'it'?

Life Skills and Values

wildlife conservation

1. Why do you think Sudan's death was symbolic?
2. *'It is said that the greatest tragedy that our world can suffer from is to watch a species disappear.'* Do you agree with this statement? Give your reasons.

Vocabulary

words related to poaching

A. Look at the underlined words in these sentences. Tick [✓] the correct meaning.

1. The hunter started to <u>stalk</u> his prey.
   a. the stem of a flower ☐ b. follow an animal quietly ☐
2. The bird was caught in a <u>trap</u>.
   a. a piece of equipment for catching birds or animals ☐
   b. a clever plan to trick someone ☐
3. Caribou and moose are some of the largest <u>game</u> in North America.
   a. an activity or sport ☐ b. wildlife hunted for sport or food ☐
4. The poacher was caught red-handed while trying to <u>traffic</u> endangered birds across the border.
   a. buy and sell illegally ☐
   b. vehicles that are on a road at a particular time ☐
5. Twenty-two forest guards <u>patrol</u> the core area of the forest.
   a. move around an area in order to make sure that there is no trouble ☐
   b. a liquid which is used as a fuel for motor vehicles ☐

phrasal verbs

Read these sentences.

By 1982, they had all been **wiped out**.

A few northern white rhinos might be **holed up** in a remote part of Africa.

The words *wiped out* and *holed up* are examples of phrasal verbs.

A **phrasal verb** consists of a main verb and an adverb or a preposition. The meaning of the phrasal verb is usually different from the meaning of the words that combine together to form the verb.

B. Fill in the blanks with the correct phrasal verbs. You may have to change the tense of some verbs.

1. After years of hard work, things were finally starting to ______________ (look up/look after) for the businessman.
2. A thief ______________ (break away/break in) last night through the window.
3. I ______________ (look into/look after) my aunt's dog when she is out of town.
4. Rohan ______________ (get back/get across) from his vacation yesterday.
5. After searching for a long time, I ______________ (give up/give in) all hope of finding the books again.
6. While making tea, we found that we had ______________ (run through/run out of) sugar.

Grammar

simple present and present continuous tenses

We use the **simple present tense** to talk about actions happening in the present, actions which happen regularly and to express general truths.

Example: At least 20,000 southern white rhinos **roam** southern Africa.

The **present continuous tense** is used for any action that is going on but which has not yet been completed. It is also used to talk about actions that will happen in the near future.

Example: Suhail **is travelling** to Kenya next week.

A. Fill in the blanks with the simple present or present continuous tense of the given verbs.

1. The language class __________ (begin) sharp at 9 a.m. every day.
2. I __________ (go) to the concert with my friends now.
3. We __________ (watch) a movie about an African safari.
4. Riddhi __________ (play) the piano beautifully.
5. It __________ (rain) every day here during the monsoons.
6. The sun __________ (rise) in the east.

simple past and past continuous tenses

The **simple past tense** is used to talk about an action that happened at a particular time in the past, or a routine action which regularly took place in the past.

Example: Sudan, the world's last male northern white rhino, **breathed** his last.

The **past continuous tense** is used to talk about an action that started and continued for some time in the past.

Example: Sudan **was suffering** from an infection in his right hind leg.

B. Fill in the blanks with the correct options.

1. I __________ (played/was playing) with my friend when the doorbell rang.
2. We __________ (drove/were driving) to Bharatpur National Park in a jeep last winter.
3. The naughty boys __________ (jumped/were jumping) in the muddy water when their father saw them.

4. The monkeys ______________________ (sat/were sitting) on the roof when we first spotted them.
5. The police ______________________ (caught/were catching) the poachers when they came out of the forest.
6. The sun ______________________ (set/was setting) over the horizon as we drove through the dusty countryside.

plural possessives

We use **possessive nouns** to show that someone owns or possesses something. Possessive nouns are formed by adding apostrophe s *('s)* to the noun.

When the noun is plural and ends with an -s, we form the possessive by adding an apostrophe after the s *(s')*.

Example: The white rhinos' mouths are wide and square.

If the noun is plural but does not end with an s, we form the possessive by adding an apostrophe s *('s)*.

Example: The **children's** toys were scattered everywhere.

For names ending in -s, we can either add an apostrophe s *('s)*, or just an apostrophe *(')*.

Example: **James's** book is the brown one.
James' book is the brown one.

C. Underline the correct option in these sentences.

1. Can you please take me to the section for (babies/babies') clothing?
2. I could not read the (building's/buildings') names from a distance.
3. I clicked many photos of my (friends/friend's) at the birthday party.
4. This store has a good collection of (mens'/men's) clothing.
5. The two (students'/students's) projects are on display in the hall.
6. I am looking for (Thoma's/Thomas's) shoes.

Study Skills

Dictionary Skills

speed word search

You know that the words in a dictionary are arranged alphabetically. We use **guide words** to quickly locate a word in a dictionary. These are given at the top of each page. The guide word on the left page is the first entry of the page, and on the right page, it is the last entry of the page.

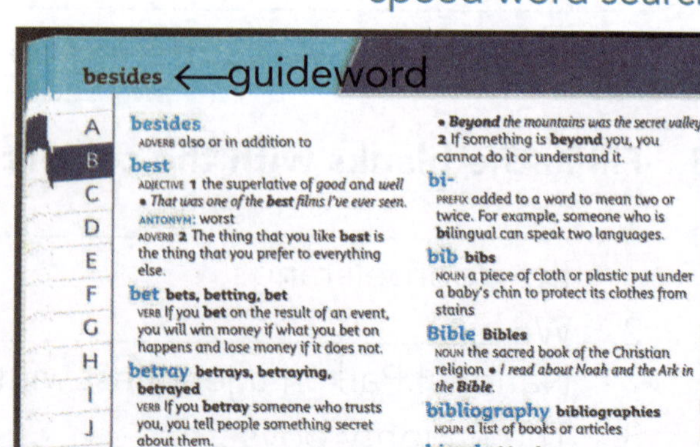
besides ⟵guideword

A B C D E F G H I J K

besides
ADVERB also or in addition to

best
ADJECTIVE 1 the superlative of *good* and *well* • *That was one of the* ***best*** *films I've ever seen.*
ANTONYM: worst
ADVERB 2 The thing that you like **best** is the thing that you prefer to everything else.

bet **bets, betting, bet**
VERB If you **bet** on the result of an event, you will win money if what you bet on happens and lose money if it does not.

betray **betrays, betraying, betrayed**
VERB If you **betray** someone who trusts you, you tell people something secret about them.

better

• ***Beyond*** *the mountains was the secret valley.*
2 If something is **beyond** you, you cannot do it or understand it.

bi-
PREFIX added to a word to mean two or twice. For example, someone who is **bi**lingual can speak two languages.

bib **bibs**
NOUN a piece of cloth or plastic put under a baby's chin to protect its clothes from stains

Bible **Bibles**
NOUN the sacred book of the Christian religion • *I read about Noah and the Ark in the* ***Bible****.*

bibliography **bibliographies**
NOUN a list of books or articles

bicycle **bicycles**

Use guide words to quickly find the meanings of these words. Then, number the words in the order that they appear in the dictionary. One is done for you.

Order	Word	Meaning
	deforestation	
	flora	
	habitat	
	ecosystem	
	organic	
1	biodegradable	(of materials) that can be broken down to a harmless natural state without harming the environment
	ozone layer	

Listening

listening for information

Listen to an excerpt of a speech given by then twelve-year-old Canadian Severn Suzuki at the Earth Summit in Rio de Janeiro, Brazil in 1992. Then, state whether the following statements are true (T) or false (F).

1. Severn Suzuki was speaking for the Economic Cultural Organization. ☐
2. The children were of the age group of six to nine years. ☐
3. Severn was speaking for the countless starving children and dying animals around the world. ☐
4. Severn was afraid to go out in the sun because of the ozone holes and harmful chemicals in the air. ☐
5. Severn said that animals and plants were growing in number every day. ☐
6. Human beings can bring back forests where there was once desert. ☐

Speaking

group discussion

Work in groups of three. One of you is the member of the Nature Club of your school. You are having a discussion with a local politician and a newspaper reporter. Discuss the importance of saving our wildlife from extinction. You can use the following points.

- our dependence on nature for survival
- every living being's right to life
- beauty and variety in nature

Writing

poster making

You read about the northern white rhinos being close to extinction. Similarly, the Great Indian Bustard, one of the largest flying birds in the world, has become an endangered species.

Create a poster about the importance of saving these birds using the given information. You may use the following points.

- state bird of Rajasthan
- current population in India: 100 (approximately)
- almost 75 per cent fall in number
- threatened by industrialization, agriculture and stray dogs
- need to preserve the grasslands where they live

Now I can... — Self-Assessment

- o read and understand an account about saving an endangered species.
- o use words related to poaching and phrasal verbs in sentences.
- o use the present and past forms of the simple and continuous tenses and form plural possessives.
- o participate in a group discussion.
- o create a poster.

Read at Leisure

***One Special Rhino—The Story of Andatu*:** This inspiring story, written and illustrated by school children from Brooklyn, USA, is about Andatu, the only Sumatran rhino to be born in captivity in Indonesia, and his fight for survival.

***Emi and the Rhino Scientist*:** This book by Mary Kay Carson is a lively account about biologist Terri Roth and her work with Emi, a Sumatran rhino at the Cincinnati Zoo.

8 The Heart of the Tree

Henry Cuyler Bunner

Reading

What can we sow to reap a rich harvest? What are the benefits of planting a tree? Read this poem to find out why planting a tree is an important deed.

What does he plant who plants a tree?[1]
He plants a friend of sun and sky;
He plants the flag of breezes free;
The **shaft** of beauty, towering high[2];
He plants a home to heaven **anigh**;
For song and **mother-croon** of bird
In hushed and happy **twilight** heard—
The **treble** of heaven's harmony—
These things he plants who plants a tree.

What does he plant who plants a tree?
He plants cool shade and tender rain,
And seed and bud of days to be,
And years that fade and flush again;
He plants the glory of the plain;
He plants the forest's **heritage**;
The harvest of a coming age;
The joy that unborn eyes shall see—
These things he plants who plants a tree.

Literary terms

1. This is an example of **refrain**, where the line is repeated in different stanzas to create rhythm.
2. This is a **metaphor**, where the poet compares the branches of the tree to a flag and the trunk to the beautiful flagpole that stands tall.

shaft: (here) a flagpole
anigh: nearby
mother-croon: low, gentle singing or humming
twilight: the time just before night when the daylight is almost gone
treble: (here) the highest notes of music
heritage: something handed down from one generation to the next

What does he plant who plants a tree?
  He plants, in **sap** and leaf and wood,
In love of home and loyalty
And **far-cast** thought of good—
  His blessings on the neighbourhood,
    Who in the hollow of His hand
    Holds all the growth of all our land—
A nation's growth from sea to sea
Stirs in his heart who plants a tree.

Food for thought

The poet uses *His* with a capital letter to indicate that the planter is like the Creator who has the power to build a nation.

sap: watery liquid in trees
far-cast: seen for the future

About the poet

Henry Cuyler Bunner (1855–1896) was an American writer who is best known for his short stories and sketches, such as *Short Sixes*, *Made in France*, and *Jersey Street and Jersey Lane*. His writings include closely observed descriptions of places and people.

Understanding the poem

A. Complete the sentences with the correct options from the brackets.

1. The poet calls the ________________ a friend of the sun and sky. (birds/tree)
2. When one plants a tree, they plant the forest's ________________ (treasure/heritage)
3. The trees planted now are the ________________ (harvest/fuel) for the generations to come.
4. A person plants a tree out of love and loyalty for his home. Here, *home* stands for ________________ (family/earth)
5. Planting a tree is also a ________________ (benefit/blessing) for the neighbourhood.

B. Answer the questions with reference to context.

1. *He plants a home to heaven anigh;/For song and mother-croon of bird*
   a. Who is 'he' in these lines?
   b. What home is the poet referring to?
   c. For whom does 'he' plant a home?
2. *A nation's growth from sea to sea/Stirs in his heart who plants a tree.*
   a. Whose heart is being referred to in these lines?
   b. How does he hold the growth of the nation in his hands?
   c. Explain the phrase 'stirs in his heart' in your own words.

Life Skills and Values

importance of planting trees

1. What are the benefits of planting a tree as mentioned in the poem? Is planting a tree an important activity for mankind?
2. The poet says that by planting a tree, a person contributes to the nation's growth. Do you agree? Give reasons for your answer.

Vocabulary

alliteration

Look at these examples of alliteration from the poem.

He plants a friend of **s**un and **s**ky

He plants a **h**ome to **h**eaven anigh

A. Underline the alliteration in the following lines.

1. And years that fade and flush again
2. Who in the hollow of His hand
3. The fair breeze blew, the white foam flew
4. In a summer season when soft was the sun
5. He bought a crooked cat, which caught a crooked mouse

B. Now write down two more examples of alliteration from the poem.

metaphor

C. You came across a metaphor in the poem. Now, complete the sentences with the correct metaphors from the box.

a stage	the Einstein of the class	a green umbrella	a bookworm
a gem of a person	a storehouse of stories	the lion's share	a fish

1. The tree was _______________ that saved us from the sun.
2. My brother is _______________, who always helps others.
3. Tia's granny is _______________
4. Shayar is so clever. He is _______________
5. Shakespeare wrote that 'All the world's _______________.'
6. Sudip is _______________. He reads three books every week.
7. Kanika must be _______________ because she swims so gracefully.
8. When we share food, Prateek always takes _______________

Activity

You have recently joined a nature club. Discuss with a friend the benefits of planting trees and write them down in the concept map.

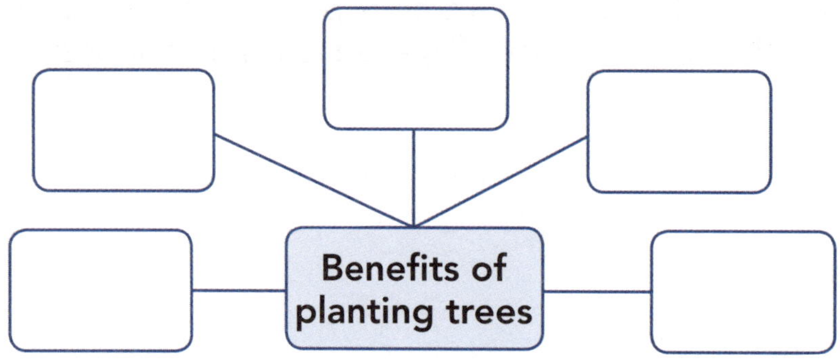

Now create your own concept map on the benefits of planting trees.

Self-Assessment

Now I can...

- understand and appreciate a poem about planting a tree.
- understand the urgency of protecting the environment.
- understand and identify alliteration and metaphors.
- create a concept map.

Read at Leisure

Tall Trees: This poem by Eileen Mathias describes trees as human beings who watch the surroundings and welcome the birds in the evening to rest.

The Apple Tree: This poem by Jane Taylor is about a boy who is tempted to steal apples from someone's apple tree.

V

Mythology

Take Off

A. Match the names of the Greek gods with their descriptions.

1. 
Zeus

2. 
Helios

3. 
Athena

4. 
Artemis

a. the goddess of the Moon and hunt

b. the king of the gods

c. the god of the sun and light

d. the goddess of wisdom, skills and warfare

B. Complete the paragraph about the Greek hero, Hercules.

Hercules was a great warrior. He completed (complete) twelve difficult tasks over twelve years. First, he ________ (fight) and ________ (defeat) the Nemean lion. Then, he ________ (kill) the Hydra, a monster that had nine heads. For his next two tasks, he ________ (catch) a sacred deer, which was believed to be swifter than an arrow, and ________ (hunt) a fearsome wild boar. He even ________ (clean) the enormous dirty stables of King Augeas. Next, he ________ (chase) off man-eating birds which had beaks of bronze. His next task took him to Crete, where he ________ (catch) a dangerous bull. After this, he ________ (capture) the flesh-eating horses of King Diomedes. As his next two tasks, he ________ (fight) a battle with the Amazons to get a belt belonging to their queen, Hippolyta, and ________ (capture) a monster's cattle. His last two tasks involved ________ (find) some golden apples and ________ (catch) a fearsome three-headed dog.

graphic story

9 Phaethon and the Chariot of the Sun

Reading

Have you ever done something to impress your friends, even though you knew it might be dangerous? Read this story from Greek mythology about a boy who wanted to ride the chariot of the Sun to impress his friends.

Phaethon was the son of the Greek sun god, Helios. Every day, Helios brought the sun up on his **fiery chariot**.

Phaethon was very proud of his father.

Why was Phaethon proud of his father?

Every morning, Helios' servants, the Hours, **harnessed** four white horses to the splendid golden chariot.

Then, Helios would leap onto the golden chariot and begin the dangerous journey across the sky.

fiery: consisting of fire or burning brightly

chariot: a two-wheeled open vehicle pulled by horses in ancient times

harnessed: fastened horses to a chariot with a set of straps controlled by the driver

hauled: pulled with effort and force
tucked: put away safely
rekindle: begin to burn again
weary: tired
boasted: talked proudly
steer: control and guide in the right direction

But Phaethon was overconfident and **stubborn**. The next morning, he climbed the chariot. As soon as he took the reins in his hands, the horses **reared** and took off.

But Phaethon soon realized he had taken on more than he could handle.

The horses knew at once that the charioteer was inexperienced. They ran **willy-nilly** along a wild and dangerous course.

What did Phaethon want to show his friends?

stubborn: determined to do what one wants and unwilling to change one's mind

reared: (of a horse) stood on its hind legs with its front legs in the air

willy-nilly: (here) aimlessly

The runaway chariot **tore across** the sky, burning a **trail** behind it. This trail is called the Milky Way.

High on Mount Olympus, Zeus, the King of the gods, saw what was happening in the sky. He **hurled** a lightning bolt at the chariot.

But the chariot tilted and Phaethon fell out and **plunged** into the River Po.

Zeus now had to complete Helios' task. He called his winged horse, Pegasus. Together, they caught up with the sweating horses.

Zeus was in a raging temper. Then he found that it was young Phaethon who had been driving the chariot. He immediately started a search for him.

Whom did Zeus ask to search for Phaethon?

tore across: moved hurriedly across, at a high speed

trail: a series of marks left by someone or something as they move along

hurled: threw with great force

rashly: hurriedly and carelessly

plunged: fell downwards at great speed

But Hermes could not find him. No one saw him ever again. Perhaps he had survived, but was hiding, ashamed. Perhaps he had died.

Phaethon's sisters were heartbroken by his death.

Comprehension

A. Complete the flow chart to show the sequence of events in the story.

1. Phaethon boasted that he could ________________ ________________ →
2. But he could not manage __________ and ________________ →
3. Zeus, the king of gods hurled ________________ ________________ →
4. Phaethon fell from ______ into ________________ →
5. Later, Zeus sent ________________ ________________ →
6. No one knew ________________ ________________

B. Answer the questions with reference to context.

1. *'Son, it is indeed an important task.'*
   a. Who said these words and to whom?
   b. What was the important task being spoken about?
   c. Why was the task referred to important?
2. *'I have to take the chariot back up into the sky, somehow.'*
   a. Who said these words?
   b. What had just happened to make the speaker say these words?
   c. Did he succeed? How was the problem solved?

Life Skills and Values

obedience and humility

1. What kind of a boy was Phaethon? Describe him.
2. Phaethon could have easily avoided his fate. What qualities, if he had had them, would have helped him do so?
3. When did Phaethon realize that he had made a mistake?

Vocabulary

collocations

A **collocation** is a set of two or more words that go together naturally. Collocations are combinations of verbs, adjectives and nouns.

Examples: Zeus **took pity** and changed them into poplar trees. (verb + noun)
Zeus was in a **raging temper**. (adjective + noun)

A. Complete the collocations using the given words.

unbearable	daily	regular	strong	weary	fertile

1. __________ exercise
2. __________ soil
3. __________ pain
4. __________ lives
5. __________ traveller
6. __________ coffee

B. Fill in the blanks using the collocations in Exercise A.

1. ______________ improves one's lifestyle.
2. In the ______________ of the Gangetic plains, crops grow in abundance.
3. My uncle is making a film on the ______________ of puppeteers in Rajasthan.
4. I have an ______________ in the lower back.
5. My father says that he needs a cup of ______________ to wake up in the morning.
6. The ______________, not finding any motel nearby, lay down under a tree and fell asleep.

Grammar

kinds of sentences

You know that there are four kinds of sentences.

An **assertive sentence** makes a statement and ends with a full stop.

Example: Phaethon was the son of the Greek sun god, Helios.

An **interrogative sentence** asks a question and ends with a question mark.

Example: Did you find Phaethon near the River Po?

An **exclamatory sentence** expresses a strong feeling and ends with an exclamation mark.

Example: How rashly Helios is driving the chariot!

An **imperative sentence** gives a command or advice or makes a request.

Example: You can take the chariot tomorrow, but remember there are dangers.

A. Identify the type of each sentence and rewrite as instructed.

1. Shalu is driving the car in the rain. (change to interrogative)
   Assertive. Is Shalu driving the car in the rain?
2. Can you please pass me the salt? (change to imperative)
3. Look how tall the Burj Khalifa is! (change to assertive)
4. March ahead, soldiers! (change to interrogative)
5. She is a successful writer. (change to exclamatory)
6. Leave at once. (change to interrogative)

modals

Modals are a type of helping verbs. They are used to talk about ability, to ask for permission, to suggest possibility, resolve and to give advice.

Some common modals are *can* and *will*, *must* and their negatives, *cannot*, *will not* and *must not*.

Examples: Only Helios **can** control the horses. (ability)
You **can** take the chariot tomorrow. (giving permission)
I **will** be as good a driver as him. (resolve)
You **must** steer the horses with a strong hand. (giving advice)

B. Fill in the blanks with the correct modals.

1. __________ (Must/Can) I play after completing my homework?
2. We __________ (will/must not) pluck flowers.
3. The robbers __________ (will/must) target the bank on Swagat Road next.
4. They __________ (cannot/must not) read Japanese.
5. __________ (Can/Must) you help me carry this bag?
6. The poor, old man __________ (must not/cannot) pay the rent for his room.

Study Skills

Pronunciation

words with *ch* and *th*

The letters *ch* and *th* can each be pronounced in different ways.

ch
- with the *k* sound as in *e**ch**o*, *an**ch**or*
- with the *sh* sound as in *para**ch**ute*, *ma**ch**ine*
- with the *ch* sound as in ***ch**ildren*, ***ch**oice*

th
- with the *th* sound as in ***th**ermos*, ***th**orn*
- with the *th* sound as in *fa**th**er*, *fea**th**er*

Read the words aloud. Then, write them in the correct columns.

chemicals	weather	chin	stomach	moustache
another	chair	thermos	chef	mouth

ch as in *mechanic*	*ch* as in *machine*	*ch* as in *children*	*th* as in *thorn*	*th* as in *father*

Listening

listening for sequence

Listen to a story about the sun and the wind. Then, number the sentences in the order of events in the story.

☐ But the traveller wrapped his cloak more tightly around himself.

☐ The one who could make a traveller on the road remove his cloak would be the winner.

- [ ] Once, the Sun and the Wind had a quarrel over who was the stronger of the two. They agreed to have a contest of strength.
- [ ] The traveller started to sweat and took off his cloak.
- [ ] The Wind chose to have the first turn and started blowing very hard.
- [ ] The Wind had to accept his defeat.
- [ ] Next was the turn of the Sun. He shone very brightly.

Speaking

conversation

Work in pairs. Enact a conversation between Helios and Zeus after Phaethon goes missing.

You may begin in this way.

Zeus: Helios, I sent for you after what happened today with the sun chariot.

Helios: Yes, Zeus. Phaethon insisted that he could ride it well.

Zeus: But he is a young boy. You should not have allowed him. Tell me what happened from the beginning.

Writing

writing an alternate ending

What do you think would have happened if Phaethon had not disappeared? Write the story of Phaethon with an alternate ending in which he survives and returns to his family. You may include these points:

- Phaethon realizes the danger of pride.
- He asks his father for forgiveness.
- He is blessed by Zeus and granted a special power.

Now I can... Self-Assessment

- read and appreciate a mythological story.
- use collocations.
- identify and transform different kinds of sentences and use modals.
- pronounce words with *ch* and *th*.
- listen to and sequence the events in a story.
- enact a conversation and write an alternative ending to a story.

10 The Labours of Hercules

Paul Perro

Reading

Have you read any stories of Greek heroes? Name a hero and say why you like the person.

Hercules is the Roman name for the Greek hero Herakles, the son of Zeus. Hercules was known for his extraordinary strength and for completing twelve 'labours' or tasks given to him by King Eurystheus, whom he served for twelve years. What did Hercules achieve when he completed the seemingly impossible tasks? Read the poem to find out.

The great warrior Hercules
Was made out of pretty **stern** stuff.
He carried out twelve famous tasks,
All of them really tough.

He fought a lion with claws so sharp
That it could rip **armour** to **shreds**.
And then he killed a **hydra**, that's
A monster with nine heads.

After that he was told to go
And catch a golden deer.
The deer was very hard to catch
It took Hercules a full year.

His next task was hunting again
This time a wild **savage** boar.
After that he cleaned a stable
Which was full of **manure**.

stern: tough and steely

armour: metal clothing that soldiers used to wear in battle

shreds: small, narrow and torn pieces of a material, such as paper, cloth

hydra: in Greek mythology, a nine-headed serpent which grew two new heads every time one of its heads was cut off

savage: wild, violent and uncontrolled

manure: animal dung

Common idioms and proverbs

clean the Augean stable: This idiom, referring to one of Hercules' labours, is used to describe a pending difficult and unpleasant task.

Hercules cleaned those huge stables
In just one single day,
And then he had to go and chase
Some nasty birds away.

Next he caught a dangerous Bull
'Twas **rampaging** through Crete.
After that he stole some horses
That had a taste for meat.

He went to the **Amazons** next
And **wound up** having a battle.
And after that he had to go
And steal a monster's cattle.

Next he had to search the whole world
To find some special magic fruit.
And finally he caught a dog,
A huge, three-headed **brute**.

Hercules earned a great reward
For being so strong and so clever;
His father Zeus promised him
That he would live forever.

rampaging: moving through a place in a violent and uncontrollable manner

Amazons: (in Greek mythology) a group of female warriors

wound up: ended up in a situation one did not plan to be in

brute: (here) a fierce and violent animal

Food for thought

Crete is the largest island in Greece. Ida Mountain in Crete is considered the birthplace of Zeus in Greek mythology.

About the poet

Paul Perro (born 1965) is a British children's writer. He has written books for children on ancient Rome and on the Greek myths. His poems retell the classic tales in a fun way.

Understanding the poem

A. Name the following from the poem.

1. The great warrior: ____________
2. Number of tasks: ____________
3. A monster with nine heads: ____________
4. The stables were full of this: ____________
5. It was rampaging through Crete: ____________
6. They fought a battle with the warrior: ____________

B. Answer the questions with reference to context.

1. *He fought a lion with claws so sharp/That it could rip armour to shreds.*
   a. Who does 'he' refer to?
   b. Why was he doing these tasks?
   c. How can we say that the lion had sharp claws?

2. *Hercules earned a great reward/For being so strong and so clever*
   a. Why did Hercules earn a reward?
   b. Why is Hercules called 'so strong and so clever'?
   c. What was the reward that Hercules got? Who gave it to him?

Life Skills and Values determination and courage

1. Hercules caught the golden deer even though it took him one year to do so. What does it tell you about him?
2. Do you agree that Hercules was a courageous warrior? Which was the task which needed him to be the bravest? Give reasons for your answer.

Vocabulary

contextual usage

A. Read the clues and find the words from the poem. Fill in the missing letters.

1. moving through a place in an uncontrollable manner: R_M_A_E
2. strict and severe: _T_R_
3. metal clothing worn by soldiers: A_ M _U_
4. the benefits that you receive for service, effort or achievement: R_ _ AR_
5. a fierce and violent creature: B_U_ _

words used as different parts of speech

Many words have the same form when they are used as different parts of speech.

Examples: After that he cleaned a **stable**. (noun)
After the surgery, her health is **stable**. (adjective)

B. Fill in the blanks with the correct words from the box. Then, tick [✓] the correct part of speech for each word.

blue	stuff	stole	live	head

1. a. Hercules was made of pretty stern stuff. — verb/noun
   b. Don't stuff too many things in one bag. — noun/verb
2. a. It is getting dark, let us __________ home. — verb/noun
   b. In Greek mythology, Medusa had snakes for hair on her __________ — verb/noun
3. a. Two of my cousins __________ in Australia. — adjective/verb
   b. We watched a __________ music concert yesterday. — verb/adjective
4. a. Can I borrow your __________? — verb/noun
   b. I don't know who __________ the ring. — noun/verb
5. a. My favourite colour is __________. — noun/adjective
   b. Will you wear the __________ jacket today? — adjective/noun

Activity

creating and describing a character

Create your own mythological character or monster. Draw it on a chart paper and colour it. Give it a name.

Include a brief description of the monster and explain why you chose the character. Show your drawing to the class and talk about it.

Now I can... — **Self-Assessment**

- read and enjoy a mythological poem.
- identify words from the poem using clues.
- identify and use a word as different parts of speech.
- create and describe a mythological character or monster of my own.

Read at Leisure

Greek Gods: This fun poem by Paul Perro introduces readers to Greek gods and goddesses and their personalities.

Pandora's Box: This poem by Paul Perro retells the story of Pandora's box.

VI

Misadventures

Take Off

A. A misadventure is an unfortunate incident, a misfortune or an unlucky event. Have you ever found yourself in a difficult situation not of your own making? Choose any one of the following situations and speak on it for two minutes. Make your story as humorous as possible.

1. You are walking on the road. You are looking upward to observe a brightly-coloured bird you have never seen before. Suddenly you look in front and see a lamppost right in front of you.

2. You have taken your dog out for a walk, when he spots the neighbour's cat. He starts growling and chasing the cat. You are dragged along behind him as you cling on to his leash.
3. You decide to surprise your parents by making them something to eat, but you mix up the sugar and salt.
4. You are on a picnic with your friends. While playing football, you kick the ball which flies through the air and hits a beehive.

B. Use the clues to complete the words related to adventure.

1. a piece of land that is completely surrounded by water — I _ _ _ _ D
2. when a ship is destroyed by storm or accident — S _ _ _ W _ E _ K
3. travelling from one place to another — J _ _ R _ _ Y
4. a collection of valuable things such as gold coins and jewels — T _ _ _ S _ _ E
5. bandits — R _ _ _ E _ _
6. to take someone away by force in order to demand something in exchange for their freedom — K _ _ _ _ P

adventure

11 Don Quixote and the Enchanted Helmet

Miguel de Cervantes

Reading

This extract is adapted from the novel, Don Quixote. *Written in the seventeenth century, it describes the adventures of the elderly nobleman Don Quixote and Sancho Panza, a farmer who becomes his squire. Quixote, having read stories of the heroic deeds of brave knights, wants to be a knight himself and perform deeds of glory. Do you think he succeeds? Read on to find out.*

Days passed and still Don Quixote rode **bare-headed**, for as yet he had found no means to win a new helmet.

One morning, as the knight and his squire were riding along a highway from a small village to a larger one, they saw a horseman coming slowly towards them.

'See there!' cried Don Quixote. 'Now I shall have an adventure that will bring me glory.'

'I pray to God, master, that it isn't like our last adventure, when you chased windmills, thinking them to be giants!' exclaimed Sancho.

Food for thought

Don Quixote was inspired by old novels about brave knights. Their adventures usually involved rescuing beautiful maidens from danger, battling ferocious dragons, or finding a treasure at the risk of their lives.

'Silence! Or I shall have you thrashed soundly. Don't you see that horseman?' said Don Quixote. 'He is wearing something on his head that glitters like gold. If I am not wrong, he is a knight, and it is Mambrino's helmet that he is wearing.'

Don Quixote had read in his books of chivalry about the Moorish king Mambrino, who owned an **enchanted** golden helmet. Anyone who wore it could never be attacked.

'Are you sure you are not mistaken, master?' Sancho asked nervously.

'Not a chance, Sancho,' Don Quixote said. 'For that knight who is riding towards us on his horse has a helmet of gold on his head.'

What did Don Quixote do in his last adventure?

bare-headed: (here) without a helmet

enchanted: having a magical quality

'I don't see any knight,' said Sancho. 'I see only a common man riding a grey donkey, much like mine. There is something bright on the top of his head; but all that glitters is not gold[1].'

'I tell you, it is Mambrino's helmet, and it is gold!' cried Don Quixote, growing angry.

Now, the smaller of two villages had no barber. The people there had to depend on the barber in the larger village, who rode over whenever he was wanted.

Sometimes he was called to **trim** the men's beards, sometimes to **dress** the ladies' hair; but he was most often needed to bleed an ailing person. For in those times, people believed that any illness could be cured by opening a vein of a sick person and letting out the 'bad' blood.

So, the barber always had a brass basin to catch the blood as it flowed from the patient's arm. This basin was always kept very clean. The knight on the galloping horse was none other than the barber riding his grey donkey to visit his patients in the smaller village.

The morning was cloudy, and it was about to rain at any minute. The barber had a new hat which he did not want to spoil in the rain. So, he had worn the brass basin upside down upon his head. It covered his hat, and being clean, glittered at more than a mile's distance.

But Don Quixote had read so much about Mambrino's helmet that he could think of nothing else. If he wanted to find a golden helmet, his mind could turn anything he wished into one.

Food for thought

Mambrino was a fictional Moorish king, who was a character in a Spanish poem. His helmet had an idol, designed such that whenever the wind blew through it, it said, 'Long live the most noble lord Mambrino, and all his barons'. Whoever wore the helmet could never be defeated.

Common idioms and proverbs

1. **All that glitters is not gold:** This proverb means that all that is attractive is not always valuable.
2. **take to his heels:** run away from somebody/something

When Don Quixote saw the poor 'knight' come nearer, he raised his **lance**, which was only the branch of a tree. Without any warning whatsoever, he charged on his mare towards the startled man. As he galloped close, he pointed the lance at him, determined to **run him through**, and shouted, '**Wretch**, save yourself or at once **surrender** the helmet, which is justly mine.'

The barber, seeing a wild-eyed old man charging at him on a horse, had just enough time to throw himself from his donkey and take to his heels[2]. He leaped over the **hedge** at the side of the road and ran away across the fields as swiftly as a deer. But the brass basin, having slipped from his head, was left lying in the dust.

Don Quixote stopped his mare. 'Here, Sancho!' he cried. 'Here is my helmet. Come and pick it up.'

trim: make neat and clean by cutting away the unwanted parts
dress: (here) to arrange hair
lance: a long spear used by a soldier on horseback
run him through: stab him
wretch: an unfortunate person
surrender: give up something
hedge: a row of bushes

'Upon my word, that is a fine basin,' said Sancho, as he handed it to his master.

Don Quixote, with great delight, **clapped** it on his head. He turned it this way and that, and tilted it backward and forward.

'It is pretty large,' he said. 'The head for which it was made must have been a big one. Sadly, it has no **visor**, and half of one side is missing.'

Sancho tried to hide his laughter.

'What are you grinning at now?' cried his master, angrily.

'Oh, nothing,' answered Sancho. 'I was only thinking what a big fool the man must have been to wear a helmet that looks so much like a barber's basin.'

'Well, it does look like a barber's basin,' said Don Quixote. 'But that is because some **enchanter** has changed its form. When we come to a town where there is an **armourer**, I will have it remade in its proper shape; for there is no doubt that it is really the helmet of the famous Mambrino.'

He turned it about on his head, and pulled it well down over his ears.

'I'll wear it as it is,' he said. 'It is better than not having a helmet.'

'There is that 'knight's' silver grey horse,' said Sancho, pointing to the barber's grey donkey which was nibbling grass by the roadside. 'I think I will exchange my own faithful beast for him.'

'Well, exchange is no robbery,' answered Don Quixote. 'We do not rob those whom we meet, for that is not what a brave knight does. The horse is no doubt very dear to its master. It should be left for him; but I give you leave, Sancho, to exchange saddles.'

What did Don Quixote plan to do with the helmet on reaching town?

'You are a wise master,' said Sancho. Without another word, he made his own poor donkey look three times better by dressing him in the barber's saddle.

Both having gained something from their adventure, the strangely dressed knight and his squire continued on their journey.

---

clapped: (here) put the basin on quickly and suddenly

visor: (here) a piece of armour at the front of a helmet to protect the eyes or the face

enchanter: someone who uses magic to put spells on people

armourer: (here) a maker of weapons

About the author

Miguel de Cervantes Saavedra (1547–1616) was a Spanish author. In his early years, he worked as a soldier and a tax collector. His most famous work is *Don Quixote*. Cervantes had a great influence on the Spanish language, which is often called 'the language of Cervantes' in his honour.

Comprehension

A. Answer the questions in a few lines.

1. What did Don Quixote see on his way to the large village?
2. Why did the barber carry a brass basin with him?
3. Why did Don Quixote attack the barber?
4. How did the barber run across the fields? What is he being compared to and what is the figure of speech used here?
5. What did the two men do when the barber left the basin behind him?
6. What exchange did Sancho want to do and why?

B. Answer the questions with reference to context.

1. *'If I am not wrong, he is a knight, and it is Mambrino's helmet that he is wearing.'*
   a. Who said these words and to whom?
   b. Who was referred to as the knight?
   c. Who was Mambrino? What was special about his helmet?
2. *The barber, seeing a wild-eyed old man charging at him on a horse, had just enough time to throw himself from his donkey and take to his heels.*
   a. Who was the 'wild-eyed old man'? What did he want from the barber?
   b. How did he charge at the barber and what did he say?
   c. What did the barber leave behind when he took to his heels?

Life Skills and Values — appreciating humour

1. Why was Sancho nervous about Don Quixote's new adventure?
2. Why did Sancho try to hide his laughter on seeing him wear the helmet?
3. Do you agree with Don Quixote's reasoning for the exchange of saddles? Give reasons for your answer.
4. Pick out three things that you found humorous in the story.

Vocabulary

proverbs

A **proverb** is a short sentence that people often quote, which gives some advice or expresses something about life in general.

Example: **Good things come to those who wait.** (*If you are patient, good things will happen to you.*)

A. Match the following proverbs with their correct meanings.

Proverbs	Meanings
1. Actions speak louder than words.	a. No one can live alone.
2. Laughter is the best medicine.	b. People who are similar spend time together.
3. No man is an island.	c. Laughter makes it easy to handle difficult situations.
4. Birds of a feather flock together.	d. It's always better to tell the truth than to lie.
5. Don't count your chickens before they're hatched.	e. What you do is more important than what you say.
6. Honesty is the best policy.	f. Don't be confident of success till you see the result.

similes

B. Fill in the blanks with the correct similes.

as nice as pie　as white as milk　like peas in a pod　as the sun
like crystal　as good as new　like a nightingale

1. The lace curtains are ____________________
2. Misti and Gunjan are best friends. They are ____________________
3. Mani is kind and friendly. He is ____________________
4. The water in the lake was shining ____________________
5. Her eyes were as bright ____________________
6. Smita sang ____________________
7. The cobbler repaired the shoe so nicely that it looks ____________________

Grammar

types of adverbs

Adverbs tell us more about verbs, adjectives and other adverbs in sentences. Let us read about the different kinds of adverbs.

Adverbs of place tell us *where* the *action* happens.

Example: 'See **there**!' cried Don Quixote.
Some more adverbs of place are *here*, *nowhere*, *everywhere* and *out*.

Adverbs of manner tell us *how* the action happens. They mostly end in *-ly*.

Example: They saw a horseman coming **slowly** towards them.
Some more adverbs of manner are *neatly*, *quickly*, *sadly* and *calmly*.

Adverbs of time tell us *when* the action happens.

Example: **Yesterday**, the knight and his squire came across a barber.
Some more adverbs of time are *today*, *tomorrow*, *recently*, *soon* and *now*.

Adverbs of frequency tell us *how often* the action occurs.

Example: Anyone who wore the helmet could **never** be attacked.
Some more adverbs of frequency are *always*, *rarely* and *sometimes*.

A. Circle the adverbs and state their types.

1. My red bag is kept there. ______________
2. He bought a new scooter yesterday. ______________
3. Please go inside. ______________
4. She drove the car carefully. ______________
5. The next train will arrive soon. ______________
6. I seldom go to the zoo. ______________

conjunctions

Conjunctions are joining words. They join two or more words or sentences.

Examples: The knight **and** his squire were riding along the highway.
'Wretch, save yourself at once **or** surrender the helmet.'

Some more conjunctions are *because*, *for*, *nor*, *but*, *yet*, *so*, *since* and *as*.

B. Fill in the blanks using the correct conjunctions.

yet as so but because or

1. I want a new cycle, ______________ I don't have the money to buy one.
2. It was raining, ______________ we decided to stay indoors.
3. He rushed to the market ______________ the shops were about to close.
4. Ragini did not get good marks ______________ she did not study well.
5. Would you like tea ______________ coffee?
6. I invited him myself, ______________ he did not come to the party.

Study Skills

Spelling

words ending in *-er* and *-or*

The spelling of words that end with *-er* and *-or* are often confused as these letters have similar sounds.
Examples: barber   author   master   collector

Read the sentences and complete the words with *-er* or *-or*.

1. The rid _____ rode his horse over the fence.
2. The bak _____ gave me a loaf of fresh bread.
3. My uncle is a swimm _____ at the national level.
4. My teacher wants me to be the monit _____ of the class.
5. The helicopt _____ flew over the forest.
6. J.K. Rowling is the creat _____ of the *Harry Potter* series.

Listening

listening for details

Listen to another extract from *Don Quixote* and fill in the blanks with the correct options.

1. The giants were actually ____________ (windmills/houses/people)
2. According to Don Quixote, the giants had long ____________ (arms/legs/heads)
3. Sancho was ____________ (amused/puzzled/scared)
4. Don Quixote felt that Sancho did not have ____________ (interest/belief/experience) in adventure.
5. Rocinante was a ____________ (donkey/horse/elephant)

Speaking

dialogue

Work in pairs to play the roles of Don Quixote and Sancho Panza. Enact the events of the story with dialogues and expressions.

Useful words and phrases

- You are wrong… can't you see
- I think that is no helmet but…
- Save yourself or surrender…
- What a coward… ran away without a proper fight
- Ah! This is a splendid helmet…

Writing

writing a funny story

Write a funny story on one of the following situations.

1. A frog leaping out of someone's schoolbag
2. Riding a horse for the first time
3. A cricket ball smashing the principal's window

Now I can... **Self-Assessment**

- read and understand a humorous story.
- understand the use of proverbs and similes.
- identify and use different kinds of adverbs, and conjunctions.
- enact a dialogue related to the events in the story.
- write a funny story on a given situation.

Read at Leisure

Beowulf: This book by Michael Morpurgo is about the legendary Scandinavian hero who saves his people from the ogre, Grendel and his even scarier mother. But he meets his match in a terrible dragon.

The Scarecrow and his Servant: This book by Philip Pullman is about the grand adventures of a knightly Scarecrow who suddenly comes to life, and a boy, Jack, who becomes his faithful servant.

adventure

12 Alone on the Island

Robert Louis Stevenson

Reading

This extract from the novel Kidnapped, *is about a seventeen-year-old Scottish boy David Balfour. After the death of his parents, David leaves his home to meet his Uncle Ebenezer. Ebenezer, a cunning man, gets David kidnapped by a ship's captain to be sold as a slave in America. Their ship is wrecked and David is washed ashore on the Isle of Erraid. Do you think David finds a way to leave the island? Read on to find out.*

The time I spent on the island is still a terrible memory for me. I had nothing in my pockets except money and Alan's silver button. I knew that shellfish were good to eat, and among the rocks I found plenty of **limpets**. There were also little shells that we call buckies or periwinkle. These made up my entire diet and I ate them cold and raw.

Food for thought

The Isle of Erraid is a tidal island about one mile square in the island group of Inner Hebrides, in Scotland. Erraid lies to the west of the island of Mull, and to the southeast of the small island of Iona. The Sound of Iona is a narrow stretch of water that connects Mull and Iona.

At first they seemed delicious. When I had them for the first time, I was **seized** with **giddiness**. For a long time, I lay on the ground feeling that I would die. But the food went down better the second time.

All day it rained. There was no dry spot to be found. That night, I went to bed between two boulders that made a kind of roof.

The second day I walked to all sides of the island. It was all **desolate** and rocky; nothing but game birds and the gulls sat on the outlying rocks. But the **creek** that separated the isle from the mainland flowed into the **Sound** of Iona. It was near this place that I made my home.

In this part of the isle, the shellfish which made up my diet grew in great plenty. The other reason for staying here went deeper.

limpets: small shellfish with pointed shells that attach themselves to rocks

seized: (here) taken over by

giddiness: a feeling of dizziness that makes you think that you are about to faint

desolate: empty of people

creek: a narrow area where the sea comes a long way into the land

Sound: (here) a narrow stretch of water that joins two larger areas of water

I could not deal with the horrid loneliness of the isle.

I kept looking around me on all sides in case I saw someone coming. From a little up the hillside over the bay, I could **catch a glimpse** of the great, ancient church and the roofs of the people's houses in Iona. Over the low country of the Ross, I saw smoke go up, morning and evening from a **homestead**. Looking at men's homes and comfortable lives kept my hopes of rescue alive.

What could David see from the hill?

The second day passed; and though I kept a lookout for boats as long as the light lasted, no help came. It rained constantly, and soon, I went to sleep. It was the height of summer, yet it rained for more than twenty-four hours, and did not clear up until the afternoon of the third day. This was a day of incidents. In the morning, I saw a red deer standing in the rain on the top of the island; but he **trotted off** upon the other side.

A little later, as I was trying to catch my limpets, I found a **guinea piece**, which fell upon a rock in front of me and rolled into the sea. I realised that this was the money I had been carrying in my pocket. There must have been a hole in it. I now had no more than two guinea pieces left. I picked up a third guinea a little after. That made a fortune of three **pounds** and four **shillings**, for a lad who was the rightful **heir** of an **estate**, and was now starving on an isle in the wild **Highlands**.

By the third morning, my clothes were beginning to rot, my stockings were falling apart, my throat was **sore**, I felt weak, and the thought of eating more of the horrid shellfish turned my stomach[1]. But the worst was yet to come.

There was a high rock on the northwest of Erraid. As soon as the sun came out, I lay down on the top of that rock to dry myself and **scanned** the sea and the Ross with interest. All of a sudden, a **coble** with a brown sail and a pair of fishermen aboard came around the corner of the isle. I fell on my knees and cried out to them.

Common idioms and proverbs

1. **turned my stomach:** (something) that makes you feel upset, sick or disgusted

catch a glimpse: see something only for a moment

homestead: a farmhouse and the land around it

trotted off: ran off with short quick steps

guinea piece: an old British coin

pounds: the unit of money used in the UK

shilling: a British coin in use until 1971, worth 12 pennies

heir: a person who rightfully inherits money or property

estate: a large area of land in the country, with a large house

Highlands: a mountainous region covering north and northwestern Scotland

sore: causing pain and discomfort in the body

scanned: looked carefully

coble: a Scottish flat-bottomed fishing boat with a single mast

They were near enough to hear me. They spoke in the **Gaelic tongue** and laughed. But the boat flew on, right before my eyes, for Iona.

I ran along the shore, crying out to them. Even after they were out of hearing, I still cried and waved to them. I wept and roared like a wicked child[2], tearing up the **turf** with my nails in **desperation**. When I was a little over my anger, I felt hungry again. I ate the shellfish even though I could barely stand it. Again, I fell terribly sick after eating. My throat was so sore I could **scarce** swallow; and I had a fit of **shuddering**.

Literary term

2. This is a **simile**. David compares himself to a child who is weeping and howling for something he wants desperately.

By the time night fell, my clothes were dry. I was much better than all the time I had landed on the isle, and I got to sleep at last.

The next day (which was the fourth) I felt very weak. But the sun shone, the air was sweet. Soon, I saw a boat coming down the Sound, in my direction. At first, I turned away. But when I looked again, the boat was still coming straight to Erraid! I ran to the seaside. My mouth was so dry; I had to wet it with seawater before I was able to shout.

It was the same boat and the same two men as yesterday. Now there was a third man along with them. As soon as they came close, they let down their sail and waited quietly. They drew no nearer.

Whom did David see on the boat on day four?

The new man laughed and stood up in the boat. He spoke to me, fast and with many wavings of his hand. I told him I spoke no Gaelic. Listening very close, I caught the word 'whateffer' several times; but all the rest was Gaelic.

'Whatever,' I said, to show him I had caught a word.

'Yes, yes,' said he, and began again as hard as ever in Gaelic. This time I picked out another word, 'tide.' Then I had a flash of hope. He was always waving his hand towards the mainland of the Ross.

'Do you mean when the tide is out?' I cried.

What was the word that told David how to leave the island?

'Yes, yes,' said he. 'Tide.'

At that I turned around and leaped back the way I had come, from one stone to another, and ran across the isle. In about half an hour I came out upon the shores of the creek. I dashed through it and landed with a shout on the main island.

Gaelic tongue: the language spoken in parts of Scotland and Ireland

turf: short, thick even grass and the layer of soil beneath it

desperation: the feeling one has in a bad situation, when one is ready to do anything to change it

scarce: (here) hardly

shuddering: trembling with fear and horror

A **sea-bred** boy would not have stayed a day on Erraid; which is only a **tidal islet**, and can be entered and left twice in a day, either dry-footed, or by wading. It was no wonder the fishermen had not understood me. The wonder was that they had guessed my mistake, and taken the trouble to come back. I had lived with cold and hunger on that island for close to one hundred hours. But for the fishermen, I might have left my bones there. Even so, I had paid dearly, being ill and barely able to walk. I have seen wicked men and fools, and I believe they both have to pay for their actions in the end; but the fools first.

sea-bred: to grow up surrounded by the sea and seafarers

tidal islet: a small island formed during low tide

About the author

Robert Louis Stevenson (1850–1894) was a Scottish novelist, poet and travel writer. His most famous works are *Treasure Island*, *Kidnapped*, and *The Strange Case of Dr Jekyll* and *Mr Hyde*.

Comprehension

A. Fill in the blanks with words from the story.

1. The creek that separated the isle from the ____________ flowed into the ____________.
2. The narrator could not deal with the horrid ____________ of the ____________.
3. On the second day, the narrator kept a lookout for ____________ as long as the ____________ lasted.
4. The narrator was on the island at the height of ____________, yet it rained for more than twenty-four hours, and did not clear up until the ____________.

B. Answer the questions with reference to context.

1. *I ran along the shore, crying out to them.*
   a. Who did the speaker cry out to?
   b. Why was he crying out to them?
   c. Whom did the speaker compare himself with?
2. *A sea-bred boy would not have stayed a day on Erraid.*
   a. What was Erraid?
   b. Why would a sea-bred boy not have stayed a day there?
   c. How did the speaker finally leave the islet?

Life Skills and Values

survival in a difficult situation

1. Why did the fishermen not help the narrator at first?
2. Do you think the narrator was a clever and resourceful person, or a fool? Give reasons for your answer.

Vocabulary

compound words

Compound words are words formed by joining two or more words.

Examples: shell + fish = shellfish
main + land = mainland

A. Choose the correct words from the box to make compound words

bird book bow brush flake box path works

1. fire__________
2. foot__________
3. lady__________
4. post__________
5. rain__________
6. snow__________
7. tooth__________
8. work__________

suffixes

A **suffix** is a set of letters that is added at the end of a word to make a new word.

Examples: I was seized with giddi**ness**.
I saw a boat coming down in my direct**ion**.

B. Make new words by adding the suffixes *-ness*, *-ous* and *-ion* to the given words. You may have to change the spelling of some of the words.

1. act
2. admit
3. adventure
4. good
5. discuss
6. fit
7. compete
8. happy
9. kind

C. Fill in the blanks with the new words formed in the previous exercise.

1. Rohit took part in a skating __________
2. The explorer leads an __________ life.

3. Rohan is quite serious about __________ and being healthy.
4. I have got __________ in St Anne's School.
5. She was filled with __________ upon seeing her brother after two years.

Grammar

present and past perfect tenses

The **present perfect tense** is used to talk about actions that started in the past and have been completed recently.

Examples: He **has lived** on the island since he was a boy.
They **have built** a new fishing boat.

The **past perfect tense** is used to talk about an action that took place in the past before another action.

Example: I leaped back the way I **had come**.

A. Fill in the blanks with the present perfect tense of the given verbs.

1. I __________ the clothes in the cupboard. (keep)
2. Abu __________ his dinner. (eat)
3. Mr Nair __________ to Japan for work. (go)
4. Rani __________ her bracelet. (find)
5. The clock __________ twelve. (strike)

B. Fill in the blanks with the past perfect tense of the given verbs.

1. He __________ home in the morning, but left before anyone woke up. (come)
2. Sheena __________ in our colony's annual cultural programme last year. (perform)
3. We __________ this film last weekend. (watch)
4. My father __________ a special dish for us last Sunday. (cook)
5. I __________ all the books in the *Harry Potter* series last year. (read)

punctuation

The common marks of punctuation are the capitalisation of letters, full stop, comma, question mark and exclamation mark.

C. Rewrite the following sentences with the correct punctuation.

1. can she speak telugu
2. we went to chennai last summer
3. no I will not go to Mumbai by train
4. you can come to my house can't you
5. the taj mahal is a famous indian monument
6. mani asked the shopkeeper to give him two pencils two erasers and one ruler

Study Skills

Dictionary Skills

guidewords

You have learnt what guidewords are in an earlier chapter. Look at the guidewords given in bold. Then, circle the word in each set which would not be on the same dictionary page.

1.	**cow-crab**	a. coward	b. co write	c. coyote	d. cram
2.	**gorilla-gourd**	a. goose	b. gosh	c. gospel	d. gossip
3.	**jet-jig**	a. jewel	b. jibe	c. jingle	d. jiffy
4.	**limestone-line**	a. limit	b. linger	c. limousine	d. limp
5.	**rag-rain**	a. raid	b. rail	c. rank	d. rainbow

Listening

listening for information

Listen to a passage from the novel *Around the World in Eighty Days* by Jules Verne and complete the sentences.

1. They took a cab at the end of Saville Row and ____________________
2. The cab stopped in front of the railway station at ____________________
3. A poor beggar woman came up to them and asked ____________________
4. Her head was covered with a bonnet, from which ____________________
5. Her shoulders were covered in ____________________ and her bare feet were ____________________
6. Mr Fogg took out the twenty guineas which he had ____________________

Speaking

conversation: asking for help

Work in pairs. Imagine yourself to be David and your partner to be one of the fishermen whom David sees. Enact a conversation in which David asks for the fisherman's help to get off the island. Take the help of the phrases from the box.

Useful words and phrases

David:	Fisherman:
Please help me!	Yes, certainly.
Would you be so kind as to...	Sure.
Could you please...	Let me see what I can do.

Writing

writing a message

Imagine that you are David. You are stuck on the island. You think of putting a message in a bottle and throwing it into the sea for someone to find. Write a message in 50 words asking for help. Include the following in your message.

- the addressee: 'Whoever finds this'
- details of the shipwreck and your current location
- your current situation (the hunger and stress, the continuous rain)
- request for help

Self-Assessment

Now I can...

- o read and appreciate an adventure story.
- o make compound words and create new words using suffixes.
- o use the present perfect and past perfect tenses and punctuate sentences.
- o ask for help and write a message.

Read at Leisure

The Coral Island: This novel by R. M. Ballantyne describes how three shipwrecked teenagers—Ralph, Jack, and Peterkin—survive on a coral island.

Treasure Island: This novel by Robert Louis Stevenson follows the adventures of Jim Hawkins as he searches for the buried treasure of an evil pirate named Captain Flint.

Project 2

A. You have read about nature in the chapters 'Sudan: The End of a Species' and 'The Heart of a Tree'. Complete the following project to bring nature into your home.

Work in groups of four. Choose three indoor plants. You can choose from the plants at home or those at your friends' homes. In class, present the following information for each plant in the form of a slide show with pictures.

- name of plant
- picture (can be a photograph or a drawing)
- description (height, shape and colour of leaves, size and colour of flowers)
- the kind of care it needs to grow
- season when it grows
- benefits of growing the plant at home

B. You have read about Don Quixote's wish to be a knight in the chapter 'Don Quixote and the Enchanted Helmet'. Now, imagine that Don Quixote meets a lady who is upset because there is a big puddle in her path. As a knight who wants to rescue 'damsels in distress', Quixote offers to help her.

Write suitable dialogue for the following cartoon strip depicting the exchange between him and the lady. Then, add four panels of your own to the strip to carry the story forward. Draw the characters to show what happens next and add dialogue. Try to make Don Quixote's new adventure as humorous as you can.

VII

Sport

Take Off

A. Work in groups of four. Choose a sport and create five clues with information related to the sport. The other groups have to guess the sport correctly, using the clues. Use the following information to create your clues for each sport.

Clue 1: number of players in a team
Clue 2: what it is played with
Clue 3: name of a famous sportsperson
Clue 4: name of an international tournament
Clue 5: name of a prominent country which plays the sport

B. Good sportspeople have some special qualities. Colour the ones that you think are important to be a good sportsperson.

goal-setter
team-player
helpful
energetic
unsympathetic
confident
cooperative
ambitious
patient
secretive
creative
fluent
fit
dependable
talented
honest
trustworthy
irresponsible
persevering
positive attitude
decisive

fantasy

13 Ron and the Lucky Potion

J. K. Rowling

Reading

This extract is taken from Harry Potter and the Half Blood Prince, *which is set in the Hogwarts School of Witchcraft and Wizardry. Harry is a young wizard, who, along with his friends Ron Weasley and Hermione Granger are students of Hogwarts. The school is abuzz with excitement as it gets ready for the annual Quidditch match between the houses of Gryffindor and Slytherin. But Ron, whom Harry had selected as the new Keeper, had played terribly during practice. Low on confidence, he is doubtful about his ability to play well in the match.*

Like Ron, have you ever felt that you might not be talented enough, in spite of others' confidence in you? Read on to see who wins the match and whether Ron gets back his confidence.

Harry knew he was right to choose Ron as the Keeper for the Gryffindor Quidditch team, but Ron was suffering from a lack of confidence and was a **nervous wreck**. Moreover, the final practice game of the season made matters worse. After letting in half a dozen goals, his technique became wilder, until he punched an incoming Demelza Robins, the Gryffindor Chaser, in the mouth.

[Ron wanted to resign from the team to save Harry embarrassment. But Harry was sure of his choice. He decided to use a ***ploy****.]*

At breakfast in the Great Hall the next morning, Hermione stopped in front of Ron and Harry.

Harry was handing Ron a glass of pumpkin juice. Hermione spoke sharply.

'Don't drink that, Ron!'

'Why not?' asked Ron.

'I just saw Harry **tip** something into the drink.'

Food for thought

Quidditch is an imaginary sport played between two teams. Each team has seven players zipping past each other on broomsticks, chasing four balls at a time: a Quaffle, two Bludgers, and a Golden Snitch.

Quidditch glossary

Quaffle: a large red ball. A team scores points by throwing it through one of three rings.

Bludger: a big iron ball which flies magically, knocking players off their broomsticks

Seeker: player who chases and tries to catch the Snitch, a golden, winged ball

Keeper: player who guards the goal

Chasers: players who get the Quaffle through a hoop at the opposing team's end of the field

Beaters: players who beat the Bludgers with short wooden clubs, toward the opposing team

nervous wreck: someone who is extremely upset and worried

ploy: plan (usually involving a trick)

tip: (here) pour something at an angle

'I don't know what you're talking about,' said Harry, putting away a little bottle **hastily** in his pocket.

Ron **drained** the glass in one gulp.
Bending low so that only Harry could hear, Hermione hissed, 'You should be **expelled** for that. I can't believe you would do that, Harry!'

The Gryffindor team was already waiting in the changing room when Ginny announced, 'The Slytherin Chaser, Vaisey is too **sore** to play! Even Malfoy is sick! They are playing Harper as Seeker instead.'

What did Ginny announce?

'*What*?' said Harry, **wheeling around**.

'Lucky, I call it,' said Ron. 'Hey!' he said suddenly, freezing and staring at Harry.

Ron had dropped his voice, looking both scared and excited. 'My pumpkin juice ... you didn't ...?'

Harry just said, 'We'll be starting in about five minutes. Get your boots on.'

Entering the pitch to loud roars and boos, Harry stepped up to Madam Hooch, the **referee**. 'Captains, shake hands,' she said, '**Mount** your brooms. On the whistle ... three ... two ... one ...' The players kicked off and Harry soared around the **perimeter** of the grounds, looking for the Snitch yet keeping one eye on Harper, zigzagging far below him.

Zacharias Smith's **jarring** voice came from the commentator's box. 'Many thought, given Ronald Weasley's **patchy** performance as Keeper last year, that he might be off the team, but a personal friendship with the Captain does help.'

'Here comes Slytherin's first attempt on goal and Weasley saves it. Well, he's bound to get lucky sometimes!'

Name the Chaser who scored the maximum goals for the Gryffindor team.

Harry grinned as he dived among the Chasers, searching for the Snitch. Gryffindor was leading sixty points to zero, Ron having made some **spectacular** saves, and Ginny having scored four of Gryffindor's six goals. This stopped Zacharias from wondering and he started on Peakes and Coote instead. 'Of course, Coote isn't the usual build for a Beater, who have generally got a bit more muscle —'

'Hit a Bludger at him!' Harry called to Coote as he zoomed past, but Coote, grinning, aimed the next Bludger at Harper instead. Harry was pleased to hear the dull *thunk* that meant the Bludger had **found its mark**.

hastily: quickly
drained: finished drinking
expelled: thrown out of school
sore: in pain
wheeling around: turning around in surprise
referee: an official who ensures that the rules of a game are followed
mount: (here) climb
perimeter: the outside edge of an area of land
jarring: unpleasant
patchy: (here) uneven
spectacular: amazing
found its mark: hit what the blow was aimed at

It seemed the Gryffindors could do no wrong as they scored again and again, and Ron saved goals with ease.

The crowd cheered with the **chorus**, '*Weasley is Our King*.'

Meanwhile Harry was nearly **knocked off** his broom as Harper **collided** with him. Though the Gryffindors below shouted in anger, the **unsporting** behaviour went unnoticed by Madam Hooch.

Harry raced after him, determined to **ram** him back.

'And I think Harper of Slytherin has seen the Snitch!' said Zacharias Smith through his **megaphone**.

Harper had spotted the Snitch speeding high above them, glinting against the clear blue sky. Harry sped up; the wind whistling in his ears, drowned the sound below. Gryffindor was only a hundred points up; if Harper got there first, Gryffindor would lose. Harper was a feet from it, his hand **outstretched** …

'Oi, Harper!' yelled Harry. 'How much did Malfoy pay you to come on instead of him?'

Harper was taken by surprise, **fumbled** and shot right past the Snitch.

Harry made a great **swipe** for the tiny, **fluttering** ball and caught it.

A **deafening** shout went up from the crowd, drowning out the whistle that ended the game. The Gryffindor team finally left the pitch arm in arm, waving to their supporters.

Ron and Harry met Hermione in the changing room.

'You **spiked** Ron's juice with *Felix Felicis* at breakfast!'

'No, I didn't,' insisted Harry.

'Yes you did, Harry, and that's why Ron saved everything!'

Why would Gryffindor lose if Harper caught the Snitch first?

Food for thought

Felix Felicis is a magic potion that Harry had received from a teacher. It brings out the best in the drinker by taking away their worry, doubt and fear. It is not allowed in any competition.

chorus: repeated lines
knocked off: thrown off balance
collided: banged into
unsporting: unfair
ram: push with force
megaphone: cone-shaped horn to make one's voice louder
outstretched: stretched out
fumbled: (here) tried to hold clumsily
swipe: swing in order to catch
fluttering: moving with quick light movements
deafening: very loud
spiked: added something without the other person knowing

Harry, grinning broadly, drew out the tiny bottle full of a golden potion with the cork still tightly **sealed** with wax. 'I wanted Ron to think I'd done it, so I faked it when I knew you were looking. Ron did it all by himself.'

Ron **gaped** at him for a moment, then **rounded on** Hermione. 'See! I can save goals without help!' he announced, walking out of the door with his broomstick over his shoulder.

sealed: closed tightly
gaped: stared with mouth open
rounded on: attacked verbally

About the author

J.K. Rowling (born 1965) is a British novelist and screenwriter. She is best known for the *Harry Potter* fantasy novels, a series of seven books that has won many awards and has also been made into a series of successful films.

Comprehension

A. Fill in the blanks with words from the story. Then number the sentences in the order of events.

The players __________ their broomsticks and Harry flew around the __________ of the Quidditch pitch. ☐

Harry caught the Snitch, and the Gryffindor supporters shouted happily. ☐

The captains of Gryffindor and __________ stepped up to __________ __________, the referee. ☐

Harry handed Ron a glass of __________ __________, which he promptly drank up. ☐

__________ __________ voice came from the commentator's box. ☐

Ron let in half a __________ goals, and punched an incoming __________ __________ in the mouth. ☐

__________ was a feet from the Snitch with his hand __________, when Harry distracted him. ☐

Harry called to __________ as he zoomed past, who grinned and aimed the next __________ at the other team's __________. ☐

B. Answer the questions with reference to context.

1. 'You should be expelled for that.'
   a. Who said these words and to whom?
   b. What does the 'that' refer to here?
   c. Do you think the speaker was excited, shocked or joking?
2. *'Yes you did, Harry, and that's why Ron saved everything!'*
   a. Who said these words?
   b. What did the speaker accuse Harry of? What reply did Harry give?
   c. What effect did Harry's reply have on Ron?

Life Skills and Values

leadership, confidence, teamwork

1. How would you describe Harry's ploy to get Ron to perform? Was he right in doing what he did as the captain?
2. Do you think that lack of confidence can affect one's performance in a sport even when someone has the ability to do well?
3. Do you agree that the Gryffindor team won because each of its members played their part? Answer with reference to the roles played by Harry, Ron and Ginny.

Vocabulary

words related to sport

A. Circle the word that does not belong to each of the following sports.

1.	**cricket**	pitch	wicket	goal	bowler
2.	**badminton**	shuttlecock	racquet	stumps	net
3.	**boxing**	wicket	wrestle	heavyweight	knock-out
4.	**football**	weights	penalty kick	defender	goal
5.	**basketball**	javelin	basket	court	dribble
6.	**hockey**	goalkeeper	volleyball	hockey stick	goal cage

homophones

There are many words that have similar pronunciations, but different meanings and spelling. These words are called **homophones**.

Example: Ginny announced, 'The Slytherin Chaser, Vaisey is too **sore** to play!'
The referee saw the golden Snitch **soar** high up in the sky.

B. Fill in the blanks using the appropriate homophones.

1. a. I tried to cheer him up, but it was in __________ (vain/vein).
   b. The nurse tried to look for the patient's __________ (vain/vein).
2. a. The girl had turned __________ (pale/pail) from the cold.
   b. The farmer filled the large __________ (pale/pail) with water.
3. a. The dress is too __________ (loose/lose) for me.
   b. If we don't act quickly, we will __________ (loose/lose) the chance.
4. a. There was a big rush in the shops due to the Diwali __________ (sail/sale).
   b. The boat lost its __________ (sail/sale) in the storm.
5. a. The train was soon out of __________ (sight/site).
   b. The engineers are inspecting the __________ (sight/site) for the new building.
6. a. Take care not to __________ (break/brake) the plates.
   b. Rohan had to __________ (break/brake) sharply to avoid crashing into the tree.

Grammar

direct and indirect speech

When we write something that someone has said using exactly the same words, it is said to be in **direct speech**.

Examples: I don't know what you're talking about,' said Harry.
'Oi, Harper!' yelled Harry. 'How much did Malfoy pay you to come on instead of him?'

When we report what someone else has said without using the exact words of the speaker, then the words are said to be in **indirect speech**.

Examples: Harry said that he did not know what Hermione was talking about.
Harry asked Harper how much Malfoy had paid him to come on instead of him. (Malfoy)

To change direct speech to indirect, we do the following.

- Remove the quotation marks.
- Change the tense of the verb.
- Use appropriate reporting verbs like *said*, *asked*, *requested*, *exclaimed*.
- Use appropriate pronouns.
- Use the conjunction *that* to introduce the reported words of the speaker.

A. Rewrite the following sentences in indirect speech.

1. 'Have you read this book?' Priya asked Vinay.
   Priya asked ______________________________.
2. 'The bus is late,' Rob said to Veronica.
   Rob told ______________________________.
3. Saima said, 'I won't be able to come for the movie since I have to visit a friend at the hospital.'
   Saima explained ______________________________.
4. 'Don't go out until it stops raining,' said Aunt Lily to the children.
   Aunt Lily advised ______________________________.
5. 'Where is the Eiffel Tower?' the tourist asked the policeman.
   The tourist asked ______________________________.
6. 'I can speak French and German,' said the teacher.
   The teacher said ______________________________.

B. Rewrite the following sentences in direct speech.

1. The little girl said that she was waiting for her mother.
   The little ______________________________.
2. The teacher advised the students not to neglect sports.
   'Do not ______________________________.
3. The prisoner insisted that he was innocent.
   The prisoner ______________________________.
4. The announcer requested the passengers to get ready for boarding.
   'Please ______________________________.
5. I asked Harry what he was doing there.
   I asked ______________________________.
6. The rabbit exclaimed that it was late.
   'Oh! ______________________________.

degrees of comparison of adverbs

Adverbs change form when they show degrees of comparison, usually by using *-er* or *-est* at the end, and sometimes by adding *more* or *most* before them.

Example: The Quaffle soared **high** in the sky.
The Bludgers soared **higher** than the Quaffle.
The golden Snitch soared the **highest** of all.

Let us look at some more examples.

hard	harder	hardest
carefully	more carefully	most carefully
little	less	least

C. **Complete the sentences with the comparative or superlative form of the given adverbs.**

quietly   hard   easily   early   beautifully   well

1. Piu solved this sum ____________ than the previous one.
2. Hiten reached the picnic venue ____________ than anybody else.
3. Neeta sang the ____________ of all the performers.
4. The librarian requested us to discuss our project ____________
5. Our cricket team played ____________ than the rival team.
6. Of all the participants, Pritam practised the ____________

Study Skills

Pronunciation

syllables

Words are often divided into parts to help us pronounce them clearly. Each part has a vowel of its own and is called a syllable. Each syllable has a single vowel sound. Say the following words aloud, saying each syllable clearly.

hand: hand (one syllable)
captain: cap-tain (two syllables)
performance: per-for-mance (three syllables)

Say the following words aloud and divide them into syllables.

1. friend
2. technique
3. referee
4. commentator
5. practice
6. confidence

Listening

listening for details

Listen to a sports commentary and answer the questions that follow.

1. Name the sport being played.
2. Who showed 'big promise' in the game?
3. What did her timing reveal?
4. What made winning the game tricky for India?
5. Which other player is mentioned in the commentary?
6. How many runs did she score?

Speaking

giving a speech

Imagine you are Harry Potter. Give a speech as the captain of the winning team after receiving the trophy. You may include these points.

- your happiness at the win
- praise for your team's efforts and special achievers: Ron's recovery and Ginny's contribution
- the turning point of the match
- special mention of the brave efforts of your opponents
- appreciating the crowd's support

Writing

informal letter

Imagine you are Ronald Weasley, who played a deciding role in the Gryffindor victory over their rivals, the Slytherins, in the Quidditch match. Write a letter to your father, discussing the excitement of the match and its special moments. You may include these points.

- your initial nervousness
- the 'lucky potion'
- Harry's faith in you and his plan
- how your sister Ginny also performed well
- the team spirit of all the players

Useful words and phrases

- During the practice match, ...
- I was feeling very sad...
- I couldn't have done this without...
- My heart stopped when Harry caught the Snitch...
- There was a loud cheer from the crowd...

Self-Assessment

Now I can...

- o read and enjoy an imaginative account of a game.
- o use words related to sports, and homophones.
- o use direct and indirect speech, and degrees of comparison of adverbs.
- o give a speech and write an informal letter.

Read at Leisure

Kid Athletes — True Tales of Childhood from Sports Legends: This collection of true stories by David Stabler talks about childhood incidents of many of today's sporting legends.

Stone Fox: This story by John Reynolds Gardner is about a young boy, his grandfather and their dog, Searchlight, whom they enter in a dogsled race.

14 A Boy Juggling a Soccer Ball

Christopher Merrill

Reading

Have you ever played football or seen a football match? What do you like about the game? Christopher Merill had a terrible experience when he was a young boy, when a hurricane swept away his family home in Seattle. After the incident, he spent countless hours practising to keep a soccer ball up in the air to take his mind off it. He was passionate about football, and years later, he wrote a poem to capture that vivid memory. Read and enjoy an extract from the poem.

... he keeps the ball **aloft** with a **nudge**
of his neck, heading it
from side to side, softer and softer,
like a dying **refrain**[1],
until the ball, slowing, balances
itself on his **hairline**,
the hot sun and sweat filling his eyes
as he **jiggles** this way
and that, then **flicking** it up gently,
hunching his shoulders
and tilting his head back, he traps it
in the hollow of his neck,
and bending at the waist, sees his shadow,
his **dangling** T-shirt, the bent
blades of brown grass in summer heat;
and relaxing, the ball slipping
down his back ... and missing
his foot[2].

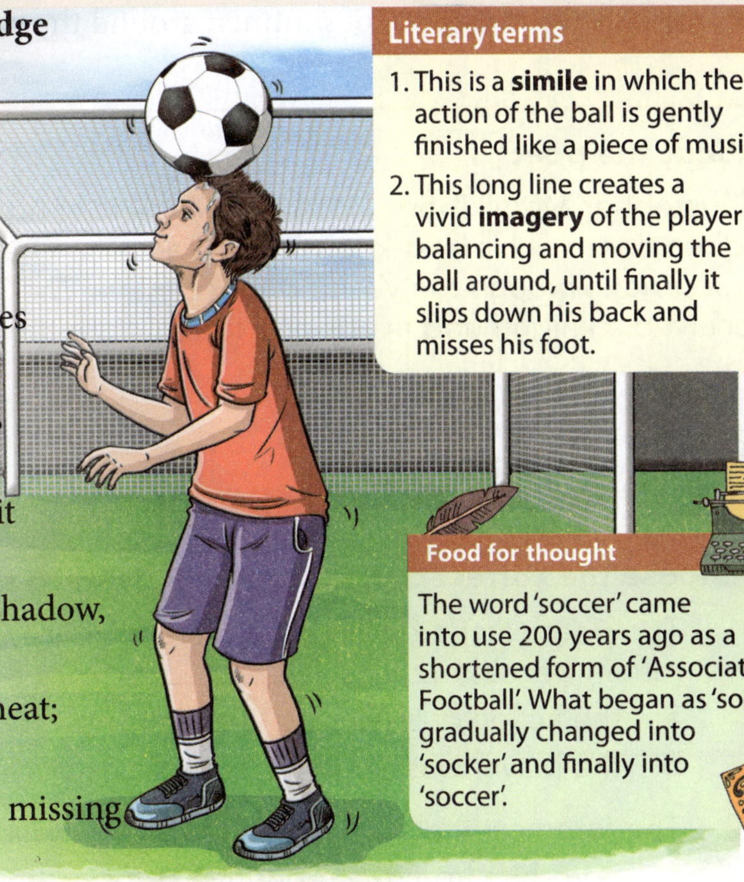

Literary terms

1. This is a **simile** in which the action of the ball is gently finished like a piece of music.
2. This long line creates a vivid **imagery** of the player balancing and moving the ball around, until finally it slips down his back and misses his foot.

Food for thought

The word 'soccer' came into use 200 years ago as a shortened form of 'Association Football'. What began as 'socca' gradually changed into 'socker' and finally into 'soccer'.

---

aloft: up in the air
nudge: slight push
refrain: a part of a song or music that is repeated
hairline: point on the forehead where the hair begins
jiggles: moves quickly from side to side
flicking: striking it quickly
hunching: bending the shoulders and leaning forward slightly
dangling: hanging loosely

He **wheels** around, he marches
over the ball, as if it were a rock
he **stumbled** into, and pressing
his left foot against it, he pushes it
against the inside of his right
until it pops into the air, is **heeled**
over his head—the rainbow!—
and settles on his **extended**
thigh before
rolling over his knee and down
his **shin**, so he can **juggle** it again
from his left foot to his right foot
—and right foot to left foot to thigh—
as he wanders, on the last day
of summer, around the empty field.

wheels: (here) circles around
stumbled: tripped and almost fell
heeled: (here) fitted/supported or tilted
extended: stretched
shin: the front part of the leg between the knee and the foot
juggle: (here) shift and balance

What does the player see in his shadow?

Food for thought

The 'rainbow' is an impressive and highly skilful move in soccer where the player uses one foot to roll the ball up the other leg, and then kick it with the opposite heel so that it flies in an arc over the head like a rainbow.

About the poet

Christopher Merrill (born 1957) is an American poet, translator, journalist and editor. Some of his best-known works are *The Grass of Another Country: A Journey Through the World of Soccer* and *The Tree of the Doves*. He has received a knighthood in arts and letters from the French government.

Understanding the poem

A. Choose the correct option to complete each sentence.

1. The poet compares the act of carefully balancing the soccer ball to a dying refrain because ____________________
   a. the action of balancing was delicately repeated like the lines of a song.
   b. the player was singing a song as he played with his soccer ball.
2. The foremost feeling that the player shows is ____________________
   a. boredom from the repetitive steps.
   b. focus and passion for a game he takes seriously.
3. The use of the word 'juggle' tells us that the player was ____________________
   a. juggling the ball like a clown in the circus.
   b. shifting the ball, and carefully balancing it from one foot to the other.

B. Answer these questions.

1. What does the initial action of the boy balancing the ball tell us about him?
2. Explain how the ball is 'heeled over' the head into a rainbow flick.
3. Which lines in the poem tell us that it was a hot summer day when the boy was practising alone?
4. Why do you think the field is empty?

C. Answer the questions with reference to context.

1. *He wheels around, he marches/over the ball, as if it were a rock*
   a. Who is the 'He' in these lines?
   b. Why do you think the poet refers to himself as 'he'?
   c. Name two literary devices that have been used in these lines.
2. *his dangling T-shirt, the bent/blades of brown grass in summer heat;*
   a. Where does the poet see his t-shirt?
   b. Why is the grass brown?
   c. Identify the alliteration used in these lines.

Life Skills and Values — determination

1. How do we know that the boy is a determined and motivated player? Pick out words and phrases from the poem to support your answer.
2. What is the poet trying to tell young readers, especially those interested in sports?

Vocabulary

forming nouns from verbs

We can form nouns from verbs by adding suffixes to them. Suffixes such as *-sion*, *-tion*, *-ation*, *-ment*, *-ance* and *-ence* are used to form nouns.

Examples: She was able to **achieve** her goals and travel all over the world.
The **achievement** of her goals allowed her to travel all over the world.

Look at the underlined verb in the first sentence in each pair. Then complete the second sentence with the noun form of the verb.

1. a. I admired the speed with which the player passed the ball across the field.
   b. I was filled with ______________ for the speed with which the player passed the ball across the field.
2. a. Anant presented his idea at the meeting.
   b. Anant made a ______________ of his idea at the meeting.

3. a. Ravi <u>performed</u> on a big stage for the first time.
   b. It was Ravi's first ____________ on a big stage.

4. a. The police <u>investigated</u> the robbery quickly, as they had only a week's time.
   b. The ____________ of the robbery was completed in a week's time.

5. a. All the members of the party <u>agreed</u> to the idea.
   b. All the members of the party were in ____________ about the idea.

Activity

article for the school magazine

Work in pairs. Imagine that you are the sports captain of your school and your partner is the editor of the school magazine. Talk about an exciting match between your school and another school. Make notes.

Now, write an article for your school magazine describing the match you just discussed. Remember to include the following in your article:

- Title: It should be short and catchy.
- Introduction: Begin with an interesting statement. Introduce the two teams.
- Body: This can be about two paragraphs describing the match. Compare the overall team performances, top players and touch upon the match highlights.
- Conclusion: Say which team finally won and what you will remember the most.
- Your name and class.

Now I can... Self-Assessment

- o read and appreciate a poem about passion and focus for a sporting activity.
- o form nouns from verbs using suffixes and use them in sentences.
- o write an article for a school magazine on an exciting inter-school match.

Read at Leisure

When Sachin Walks Out to Bat: This poem by Ruskin Bond describes the famous cricketer's moves and techniques on the field.

An Athlete's Poem: This poem by Lei Strauss describes the hard work and determination that an athlete puts into training as he dreams of winning the medal in a championship.

VIII

Art and Culture

Take Off

A. Look at the pictures of these classical musicians and the instruments they play. Identify them and the instruments.

1. Musician: ____________
   Instrument: ____________

2. Musician: ____________
   Instrument: ____________

3. Musician: ____________
   Instrument: ____________

4. Musician: ____________
   Instrument: ____________

B. Match the descriptions of the types of paint with their names.

Description	Type of paint
1. These colours look like sticks and are waxy or powdery in nature. Usually they are the first colours used by children.	a. poster colours
2. These are colours used on placards or posters. These are also mixed with water, but they dry to give a matte effect.	b. acrylic paint
3. This is a type of slow-drying paint that has oil as a base. It gives a glossy effect to paintings and many famous painters prefer it.	c. watercolours
4. This is a fast-drying paint which is water-soluble, but becomes water-resistant when dry. It is used for crafts or in art classes.	d. pastel crayons
5. These are water soluble colours and give a transparent effect to paintings. They are one of the most commonly used colours.	e. oil paint

The answers are given at the end of the chapter.

short story

15 The Concert

Shanta Rameshwar Rao

Reading

Do you play a musical instrument? Do you think music plays an important role in our lives? Read this story about two siblings who share a love for the sitar.

One morning, in a small apartment in Bombay, a girl of about sixteen looked up from her newspaper and said excitedly, 'Pandit Ravi Shankar is playing tomorrow at the Shanmukhananda **Auditorium**.'

'Sh-sh,' said her mother pointing to the figure sleeping on the bed. 'You'll wake him up. You know that he needs all the rest he can get.'

But the boy on the bed was not asleep. 'Pandit Ravi Shankar!' he said. 'Pandit Ravi Shankar, the sitar **maestro**?'

He raised himself up on his elbows for one second, then fell back. But his eyes were shining. 'We mustn't miss the chance,' he said. 'And... I... always wanted to hear him and see him.'

'Lie down, son. Lie down.' His mother **sprang** to his side. 'He actually raised himself up without help,' she **murmured** with a catch in her throat.[1] The prayer, which she **uttered** endlessly, came **unbidden** to her lips.

'I must hear him and see him,' the boy repeated. 'It's the chance of a lifetime.[2]'

Then he began to cough and gasp for breath and had to be given oxygen from the cylinder that stood under the bed. But his large eyes were fixed on his sister.

Common idioms and proverbs

1. **catch in one's throat:** a feeling that one is unable to speak due to sadness, anxiety, or another strong emotion
2. **chance of a lifetime:** This refers to an opportunity so great that it is likely to come only once in life.

auditorium: the part of a concert hall in which the audience sits

maestro: a skilled and well-known musician or music conductor

sprang: moved suddenly and quickly

murmured: said quietly

uttered: said

unbidden: without having been called

Smita bit her lip.[3] She had been so excited on seeing the announcement that she had not remembered that her brother was very ill.

She had seen how the doctors had shaken their heads **gravely** and spoken words that neither she nor her parents could understand. But somewhere deep inside, Smita had known the frightening truth. The word 'cancer' had hung in the air—even though she pretended that all would be well and they would return together, a small family of four, to their home in Gaganpur.

Food for thought

Pandit Ravi Shankar was an Indian musician and a composer of Hindustani classical music, who played the sitar. Ustad Allarakha Qureshi was an Indian tabla player. He used to accompany Ravi Shankar often on the tabla. Their interplay or *jugalbandi* was well-known.

Anant was only fifteen, and the best table tennis player in the school and the fastest runner. He was learning to play the sitar; they were both taking sitar lessons, but Anant was better than her in many other things. He was already able to compose his own tunes to the astonishment of their guru. Then they had come to know of Anant's illness and they had come to Bombay so that he could be treated at the hospital in the city.

Common idioms and proverbs

3. **bite one's lip:** to stop oneself from saying something or from showing an emotion

How old was Anant and what was he suffering from?

Whenever they came to Bombay, they stayed with Aunt Sushila. They had come with high hopes in the miracles of modern science. They told themselves that Anant would be cured at the hospital and he would again walk and run and take part in the **forthcoming** table tennis tournament.

And he would play the sitar—perhaps be a great sitarist one day. But his condition grew worse and soon the doctor at the hospital said, 'Take him home. Give him the things he likes. **Indulge** him.'

They knew then that the boy had not many days to live. But they did not voice their fears. They laughed and talked and surrounded Anant with whatever made him happy. They fulfilled his every need and gave him whatever he asked for. And now he was asking to go to the concert.

'When you are better,' his mother said. 'This is not the last time they are going to play.'

Smita stood at the window looking at the traffic, her eyes wet with tears. Her mother whispered, 'But you, Smita, you must go. Your father will take you.'

Who would accompany Smita to the concert?

When she was alone with Aunt Sushila, Smita said in a **choked** voice, 'No, how can I? We've always done things together.'

Suddenly, a daring thought came to her and she said to herself, 'Why not? There's no harm in trying it.'

---

gravely: in a serious and worried manner
forthcoming: going to happen soon
indulge: (here) give someone what they want or enjoy
choked: upset; about to cry

'It would be nice to go to the concert. I don't know when we'll get another opportunity to hear Pandit Ravi Shankar,' she said to her mother later. Her father agreed to get the tickets.

The next day, as Smita and her father were leaving for the concert, her brother smiled and said, 'Enjoy yourself. Lucky you!'

Sitting beside her father in the **gallery**, Smita heard as in a dream, the thundering welcome the audience gave the great master. Then the first notes came over the air and Smita felt as if the gates of a land of enchantment and wonder were opening. Spellbound, she listened to the unfolding ***ragas***, the slow **plaintive** notes, the fast twinkling ones, but all the while the plan she had decided on the evening before remained firmly in her mind. 'The chance of a lifetime!'

She heard Anant's voice in every beat of the tabla.

What could Smita hear in the beats of the tabla?

The concert came to an end and the audience gave the artists a standing **ovation**.

A large mustachioed man made a long speech. Then came the presentation of **bouquets**.

Then more applause and the curtain came down. The people began to move towards the exits.

Now was the time. Smita **wriggled** her way through the crowds towards the stage. Then she went up the steps that led to the **wings**, her heart beating loudly. In the wings, a small crowd had gathered to talk about the evening concert, to help carry bouquets and teacups and instruments.

He was there, standing with the man who played the tabla for him—the great **wizard** of music, Ustad Allah Rakha. Her knees felt weak, her tongue dry. But she went up, and standing before them, her hands folded, 'Oh sir,' she burst out.

'Yes?' he asked questioningly, but kindly.

And her story came pouring out, the story of her brother who lay sick at home and of how he longed to hear him and the Ustad play.

'Will you come to Aunt Sushila's house and play for him?' she asked at the end breathlessly.

'Please,' she begged. 'Please come.'

'Little girl,' said the mustachioed man who had made the long speech. 'Pandit*ji* is a busy man. You must not bother him with such requests.'

gallery: (here) an area in a concert hall high above the ground

ragas: traditional patterns of notes used in Indian music

plaintive: sounding sad

ovation: a lot of clapping from an audience

bouquet: bunch of attractively arranged flowers

wriggled: moved through a narrow space by turning and twisting the body

wings: (here) the space on both sides of the stage that the audience cannot see

wizard: (here) an expert in something

But Pandit Ravi Shankar smiled and **motioned** him to be quiet. He turned to Ustad Sahib and said, 'What shall we do, Ustad Sahib?'

'Tomorrow morning, we perform for the boy—yes?' the Ustad replied.

'Yes,' Pandit*ji* replied. 'That's settled then.'

It was a very excited Smita who came home late that night. Anant was awake, breathing the oxygen from the cylinder.

'Did you—did you hear him?' he whispered.

'I did,' she replied. 'And I spoke to him and he'll come tomorrow morning with the tabla ***ustad*** and they will play for you.'

The following morning, Aunt Sushila's neighbours saw two men get out of a taxi which **pulled up** outside their block. They could not believe their eyes.

'Is it ... It's not possible!' they said.

Pandit Ravi Shankar and Ustad Allah Rakha went up the wooden staircase and knocked softly on the door of Aunt Sushila's apartment. They went in, sat down on the **divan** by the window and played for the boy, surrounding him with a great and beautiful happiness as life went out of him, gently, very gently.

(This is a true story, but all the names except those of Pandit Ravi Shankar and Ustad Allah Rakha have been changed.)

motioned: made a gesture with his hand

ustad: an expert or a highly skilled person, especially a musician

pulled up: slowed down and stopped

divan: a bed with a thick base under the mattress

Comprehension

A. State whether the following statements are true (T) or false (F). Correct the false statements.

1. Smita was excited because Pandit Ravi Shankar was going to perform the next day. ☐
2. Smita bit her lip because she wished to go to the concert alone. ☐
3. Anant was so ill that he had to be given oxygen from the cylinder. ☐
4. Anant was the best tennis player in the school. ☐
5. Aunt Sushila's neighbours were surprised to see a van arrive in the neighbourhood. ☐
6. Pandit Ravi Shankar and Ustad Allah Rakha did not pay any heed to Smita's pleas. ☐

B. Answer the questions in a few lines.

1. Why could Anant not go with Smita to the concert?
2. Why did the family go to Bombay?
3. What were the things Anant was good at?
4. How did Smita feel at the concert?
5. What did Smita ask of Pandit Ravi Shankar?
6. Why could Aunt Sushila's neighbours not believe their eyes?

C. Answer these questions with reference to context.

1. *'It's the chance of a lifetime.'*
   a. Who said these words and to whom?
   b. What was 'the chance of a lifetime'?
   c. Describe the truth that is hidden in these lines.
2. *'That's settled then.'*
   a. Who said these words and to whom?
   b. What was settled?
   c. What do these words tell us about the speaker?

Life Skills and Values — love between siblings, compassion

1. Did Smita love her brother? Explain with examples from the story.
2. Why did Smita hear Anant's voice in every beat of the tabla?
3. What quality did the two musical maestros show? Explain with examples.

Vocabulary

forming adjectives from verbs

We often add *-d* or *-ed* to verbs to form adjectives. An adjective that ends in *-ed* is usually used to describe a feeling or an emotion.

Examples: choke ⟶ choked
disgust ⟶ disgusted

Fill in the blanks with the adjective form of the given words.

bore	disappoint	confuse	shock
annoy	relax	tire	worry

1. Sheena had a ________________ expression as she did not have anything to do.
2. The teacher was ________________ with the noisy class.
3. Somesh looked ________________ when he read the question paper.

4. Don't be ________________. You will do better in the next round.
5. I can't find my watch. Now I am really ________________
6. The crowd was ________________ to hear the news of the earthquake.
7. Tuhina looked so ________________ after meditation.
8. Tehmina felt ________________ after a long day.

Grammar

irregular verbs

Some verbs are irregular in form. They do not end in *-ed* in the past tense.

Examples: spring ⟶ **sprang** go ⟶ **went**
know ⟶ **knew** begin ⟶ **began**

A. Fill in the blanks with the simple past tense of the given irregular verbs.

1. I ________________ (choose) the red car.
2. The boy ________________ (drink) all the juice in the glass.
3. Sameer ________________________ (bring) a cake to the party.
4. The birds ________________ (fly) to their nests.
5. We ________________ (hear) the news on the radio.
6. Father ________________ (drive) slowly through the rain.

prepositions

Read the sentences.

Pandit Ravi Shankar is playing **at** noon tomorrow. (indicates time)

But the boy **on** the bed was not asleep. (indicates place)

The people began to move **towards** the exit. (shows movement)

The words *at, on, towards* are examples of prepositions.

Prepositions are words or group of words that show the relation between two things.

B. Fill in the blanks with the correct prepositions.

at over beneath beside in around in front of on

1. Minty is sitting ________________ her father.
2. I will go to the market ________________ Saturday.

3. As I stepped off the boat, I was happy to feel the ground ________________ my feet.
4. The cat went ________________ the garden in search of food.
5. My grandfather will visit us ________________ June.
6. I will meet you ________________ 8 a.m. sharp.
7. The dog jumped ________________ the fence.
8. The car was parked ________________ the gate.

Study Skills

Pronunciation

words with *ea*

Look at these pronunciations of words with the letters *ea*.

- with the *ea* sound, as in *hear*, *ear*
- with only the long *e* sound, with the *a* remaining silent, as in *repeated*, *defeat*
- with the short *e* sound, as in *breath*, *heavy*

Read these words aloud and write them in the correct columns.

neat bread spread clear beach dear
head reach tread near feast

ea as in breath	*ea* as in defeat	*ea* as in hear

Listening

listening for facts

Listen to a passage about Pandit Ravi Shankar and answer the questions.

1. With whose dance group did Ravi Shankar travel as a boy?
2. Who taught Ravi Shankar how to play the sitar?
3. Where did he work as a music director?
4. Name two national awards that he has won.
5. In which parts of the world had he performed?

Dictation

Listen to a passage about the sitar and write it down. Each sentence will be repeated twice. Listen carefully and try to avoid any spelling mistakes.

Speaking

making preparations

Smita and her mother are preparing for Ravi Shankar and Ustad Allah Rakha's visit to their house. Work in pairs and complete the conversation.

Smita: Oh mother, I can't believe they are actually coming! Should I place some chairs in Anant's room?

Mother: Yes, I think we should do that.

Smita: Will we prepare some snacks for our guests?

Mother: Of course. I was thinking of serving *vada pao* and *poha* along with tea.

Useful words and phrases

- Shall we...?
- I think we should...
- Let us...
- That's a great idea...
- Why don't you...?
- Can we...?

Writing

letter writing

Write a letter to the principal of your school requesting for leave to participate in a classical music concert in another city. Remember to include these elements.

- date of writing the letter
- name and designation of the person you are writing to
- salutation: 'Respected sir/madam'
- subject: one-line description of what the letter is about
- body of the letter: reason for your request
- closing: 'Yours sincerely' followed by your name

Now I can... **Self-Assessment**

- o read and appreciate a short story about the love between two siblings.
- o form adjectives from verbs by adding *–ed*.
- o form the simple past tense of irregular verbs and use prepositions correctly.
- o make preparations for welcoming guests.
- o write a letter to the principal.

Read at Leisure

Beezus and Ramona: This book by Beverley Cleary is a humorous portrayal of the ups and downs in the lives of two sisters.

The War That Saved My Life: This book by Kimberly Brubaker Bradley is a moving story of triumph against all odds set during World War II, featuring Ada and her little brother, Jamie.

Answers to Take Off:

A. 1. Hariprasad Chaurasia, flute 2. Shivkumar Sharma, santoor
3. Zakir Hussain, tabla 4. Amjad Ali Khan, sarod

B. 1. d 2. a 3. e 4. b 5. c

16 Art Is Hard

Gareth Lancaster

Reading

Art is an expression of a person's thoughts and feelings. Have you ever tried to express yourself through any form of art, such as painting, dance or acting, or do you think it is very difficult to do so? Read this humorous poem about someone who finds art difficult.

Painting's really difficult,
With pencils I'm **nonplussed**.
Charcoal just gets everywhere,
And crayons are a **bust**.

Pastels are too tricky,
And pens, they lead to **splodge**.
Gluing's just too sticky,
Papier-mâché I just **bodge**.

Art is really **taxing**,
This creating tires me out.
And I'm really far too messy,
Of that I have no doubt.

So there's paint upon the ceiling,
And pencil on the chair.
There's pastel dust just everywhere,
Mum's **shrieking** with **despair**.

Our dog's stuck to his basket,
Crayon **scrawled** across the door.
I think it will be quite a while,
'till I create once more!

Food for thought

Papier-mâché is a substance made from layers of paper pulp mixed with glue and pressed and moulded to form masks and decorative things.

nonplussed: confused and unsure how to react
charcoal: (here) a soft, stone-like black substance used to draw with
bust: a thing that is total failure
splodge: a large uneven liquid mark or stain
bodge: spoil, to make a mess of
taxing: demanding a lot of effort
shrieking: screaming
despair: total loss of hope
scrawled: drawn carelessly

Understanding the poem

A. Answer the questions.

1. What, according to the speaker, 'gets everywhere'?
2. What was the speaker quite sure of in the third stanza?
3. What were some of things that made the speaker's mother 'shriek with despair'?
4. What does the author find 'taxing'? Write down the line which suggests that he feels tired.
5. What is the possible age of the speaker—less than six years/about ten years/ above fourteen years? Give reasons for your answer.

B. Answer the questions with reference to context.

1. *Painting's really difficult/With pencils I'm nonplussed.*
   a. What does the speaker find difficult?
   b. Which word does the speaker use to show his confusion?
   c. What else does the speaker try to use apart from pencils?
2. *Pastels are too tricky/And pens, they lead to splodge*
   a. Why do you think the speaker finds pastels 'tricky'?
   b. What problems do the pens cause?
   c. Give another word for 'splodge'.
3. *Our dog's stuck to his basket/Crayon scrawled across the door.*
   a. Why do you think the dog is stuck to the basket?
   b. Why are there crayon markings on the door?
   c. What did the speaker decide as a result of his misadventures?

Life Skills and Values — understanding and appreciating creativity

1. What was the young speaker quite sure of not trying for a long time? Do you think that was a good decision?
2. Do you think creativity should be encouraged in all subjects, including mathematics and science? Why?

Vocabulary

words related to painting

A. Rearrange the letters of the jumbled words and fill in the blanks. All the words are related to painting.

1. The artist made a wonderful ________________ (KESTCH) of the girl.
2. This was my first painting on a ________________ (VASCAN).

3. The painter decided to paint a ________________ (DLANSCAEP) after looking at a beautiful view of the rising sun in the countryside.
4. Sameer made a ________________ (RPOTRAIT) of his grandmother.
5. I squeezed out some oil paints on my colour ________________ (PALEETT).
6. The ________________ (ULLSITRATIONS) in the storybook looked magical.

words of foreign origin

Papier-mâché is a French word which actually means 'chewed-up paper'. Look at some more foreign words used in everyday English.

Foreign Words	Language	Meaning
bric-a-brac	French	small inexpensive things
fest	German	celebration/festival
mammoth	Russian	very big
ketchup	Chinese	tomato sauce
plaza	Spanish	open space or square
tsunami	Japanese	huge sea wave

B. Fill in the blanks using the words of foreign origin you just read.

1. The ________________ destroyed all the hotels near the sea shore.
2. The Annual School ________________ is held in December.
3 I have a box filled with ________________ which I have collected over the years.
4. I added onions and some ________________ to the burger.
5. Rearranging all the books in the library will be a ________________ task.
6. We went to the new shopping ________________ to buy clothes for the wedding.

Activity

writing a report

Imagine that an inter-school art exhibition was organized in your school. Many beautiful artworks created by students of different schools in different mediums were displayed in the exhibition. Prizes were given to the three best paintings.

Write a report for your school magazine about the art exhibition. Give a title to the report. You can include the following points:

- details of date, time and venue
- themes
- quality of entries
- judges
- winners
- prize distribution

Self-Assessment

Now I can...

- o recite and understand a poem about art.
- o understand and use words related to art.
- o recognize and use some foreign words used in everyday English.
- o write a report about a school event.

Read at Leisure

Practising Scaring: This poem by Gareth Lancaster is about the way children can laugh off their fears.

Arthur the Artist: This humorous poem by Kenn Nesbitt is about a boy named Arthur whose works of art are painted all over his body!

IX

Science and Technology

Take Off

Every scientific invention that seems common today was once only an idea that a brilliant scientist thought of and turned into reality.

A. Match the scientists with the discoveries and inventions they are known for.

Scientists	Things they are famous for
1. Alexander Graham Bell	a. pasteurization
2. Isaac Newton	b. telegraph
3. the Wright brothers	c. electricity
4. Samuel Morse	d. computers
5. Benjamin Franklin	e. gravity
6. Marie Curie	f. aeroplane
7. Louis Pasteur	g. television
8. Charles Babbage	h. radium
9. John Logie Baird	i. telephone

Do you know the difference between an invention and a discovery? An invention is the creation of something absolutely new. A discovery is the finding of something that already existed but was not known of. The invention of the space shuttle, for example, has led to discoveries about the moon and other planets near the Earth.

B. Write whether the following are discoveries or inventions.

1. the Earth being round ____________________
2. computers ____________________
3. X-ray machine ____________________
4. wheel ____________________
5. fire ____________________
6. fountain pen ____________________
7. oxygen ____________________
8. light bulb ____________________

17 Nikola Tesla: The Forgotten Inventor

Reading

Have you ever thought of a world where things which we take for granted, such as electricity, the telephone and medicines, did not exist? Our civilization stands on the achievements of scientists who developed these. Nikola Tesla was one such person. Read on to find more about him.

Nikola Tesla

We all know about Thomas Alva Edison, the inventor of the electric bulb, but few know of Nikola Tesla today. He was a **contemporary** of Edison and many thought him to have been the greater scientist of the two. Tesla's discoveries were far ahead of his time. He is best remembered today for his invention of alternating current (AC), the form in which electricity is supplied to us.

Tesla was born on 10 July 1856, in Croatia, Europe. The fourth child of Milutin Tesla, a priest, and Djuka Tesla, he grew up to be the 'child of light' his mother had **foreseen** him to be. The story goes that a lightning storm was raging outside the day he was born. The **midwife** had said, 'He will be a child of the storm'. But Tesla's mother had replied, 'No, he will be a child of the light'. Though untaught, Djuka herself invented household **appliances** and Tesla may have **inherited** his talent for mathematics from her.

Who called Tesla 'a child of the light'?

From his early years, it was clear that Tesla was different from the rest. He was so smart that his teachers thought he was cheating on the sly.[1] After completing his school education in 1875, he went to study engineering at the Austrian Polytechnic, where he worked from 3 a.m. to 11 p.m. all week. His teachers once wrote to his parents saying that he might die of overwork. In his day-to-day life, Tesla followed a strict routine. Though he scored the highest in the first year of college, he developed a **gambling** habit. He not only lost his **scholarship** to it, but his **allowance** as well, and could not **graduate** from the university.

Common idioms and proverbs

1. **on the sly**: This idiom means to do something secretly, often because it is wrong or bad.

contemporary: someone living at the same time
foreseen: knew before it happened
midwife: woman who helps during childbirth
appliances: gadgets
inherited: (here) received a quality from parents
gambling: playing games of chance for money
scholarship: money granted for a student's education by any organization
allowance: (here) pocket money
graduate: pass out of college after getting a degree

The Niagara Falls

Tesla grew up to be a handsome young man, who always dressed fashionably. His **photographic memory** helped him to memorise entire books and calculate difficult mathematical problems in his mind. He spoke eight languages, including Serbo-Croatian, Czech, English, French, German, Italian and Latin.

He studied electricity and dreamt of designing new methods of supplying electricity to cities and homes.

Which languages could Tesla speak?

After finishing his studies, Tesla worked as an electrical engineer in a telephone company for a time. At the age of 28, he left for the United States to work for Thomas Edison's company. Edison hired Tesla to improve many of the machines he had invented. However, the arrangement did not work out and Tesla left the company. He developed the idea of alternating current. Unlike direct current (DC), which Edison had invented, alternating current made it possible to transfer huge amounts of energy over large areas. He was now working against his former **mentor**, and their differences came to be known as the 'War of Currents'.

Tesla worked with a 'Do Not Disturb' board outside his workspace. But he would call his friends at any hour of the day to share a **groundbreaking** solution to a problem. With many inventions to his name, he had as many as 112 **patents** in the USA. He also made huge **contributions** to wireless technology and X-rays. A lot of his work which was not taken seriously in his time is used today in the fields of **robotics** and **remote** control technology.

In 1891, Tesla gifted the world the Tesla coil. Believing that the Earth itself can generate electricity, he used two coils to create sparks. This resulted in huge, spell-binding lightning bolts. Tesla discovered that he could send and receive powerful radio signals through the coils. He planned to send a signal 50 miles away, but disaster struck when his laboratory, along with his work, burnt down. A few years later, Italian inventor Guglielmo Marconi, who was also working on radio waves, used Tesla's device to transmit signals across the English Channel and instead got the patent for inventing the radio. In spite of the setback, Tesla declared, 'I don't care that they stole my idea… I care that they don't have any of their own.'

Tesla coils

Years later, he designed the first ever hydroelectric plant that **generated** power from the Niagara Falls and lit up New York City. It was a historic moment.

---

photographic memory: a memory that lets a person remember things in exact detail after seeing them only for a short time

mentor: guide

groundbreaking: new and important

patents: legal rights to make or sell new products

contributions: something you do that helps to make a thing successful

robotics: the science of designing and making robots

remote: from a distance

generated: produced

Tesla planned to build a giant tower in New York which could send wireless signals and would be more powerful than Marconi's invention. Though he found people to pay large sums to set it up, the plan did not work. Those who had given him money left the project. This was the beginning of Tesla's slide into poverty. He continued developing new inventions, but it never matched the fame and wealth his earlier work had brought him. Eventually he went **bankrupt** and managed with indirect help from his earlier **investors**.

Nikola Tesla in his laboratory

Though Tesla never married, he dreamt of a world where women would one day hold equal rights and jobs as men. But many people thought him to be **eccentric** because of his fear of dirt and germs, and of the number 3!

Which inventor beat Tesla in getting the radio patent?

Nikola Tesla spent his last years in a hotel in New York, leaving his room only to feed the pigeons he loved. He would often bring them back to his room to care for them, leading to complaints from the hotel staff. Tesla died on 7 January 1943, at the age of 86, in New York, where he had lived for nearly 60 years. Nicola Tesla's imagination knew no bounds[2] and we owe a lot to this genius inventor who played a big role in shaping the world as we know it today.

Common idioms and proverbs

2. **knew no bounds:** was without limit or restriction

bankrupt: someone who does not have enough money to pay their debts

investors: people who put money in a project or business to earn profits later

eccentric: strange

Comprehension

A. Fill in the blanks with words and phrases from the passage.

1. Tesla's best known invention was ____________________
2. Tesla was born on ____________________
3. Tesla's school teachers were concerned that ____________________
4. Tesla worked at a ____________________ company.
5. The number of patents Tesla had in the USA was ____________________
6. In the year ____________________, Tesla invented the Tesla coil.

B. Answer the questions with reference to context.

1. *He grew up to be the 'child of light' his mother had foreseen him to be.*
   a. Who does 'he' refer to and what was his mother's name?
   b. What quality did 'he' inherit from his mother?
   c. How did he show in his later life that he was indeed a 'child of light'?

2. *He was now working against his former mentor, and their differences came to be known as the 'War of Currents'.*
    a. Who does the 'mentor' refer to?
    b. What work was Tesla doing for this 'mentor' earlier?
    c. Why was he 'now working against his mentor'? Why was it called the 'War of Currents'?

3. *'I don't care that they stole my idea … I care that they don't have any of their own.'*
    a. Which 'idea' was the speaker referring to?
    b. Who stole his 'idea'?
    c. What was the disaster that set Tesla back from proving his own idea?

Life Skills and Values — determination, strength of character

1. Often scientists like Tesla are called 'eccentric'. Do you think this quality is important in an inventor or a genius?
2. Tesla continued to develop new inventions even when he faced bankruptcy. What does this say about his character?

Vocabulary

words related to science

A. Find ten words related to science in the grid and circle them.

L	W	O	L	Y	U	A	K	E	T	E	I
A	D	I	S	C	O	V	E	R	I	E	S
B	A	C	E	H	L	O	P	X	M	D	Z
O	N	H	J	Q	W	P	I	U	A	I	H
R	O	B	O	T	I	S	R	C	R	S	D
A	J	T	B	D	R	M	S	O	C	O	K
T	K	I	N	V	E	N	T	I	O	N	I
O	F	Q	W	E	L	R	U	L	N	C	L
R	C	U	R	R	E	N	T	W	I	O	K
Y	L	T	P	C	S	J	I	Z	X	N	H
T	R	Y	B	H	S	G	Y	P	L	I	A
F	O	T	E	C	H	N	O	L	O	G	Y

A **word family** is the base form of a word and its derived forms made by adding letters like *-es, -ed, -ing, -er, -able, -ly, -ic, -est* and *-ist.*

Examples:

B. Write any three derivatives of these words to complete the word families.

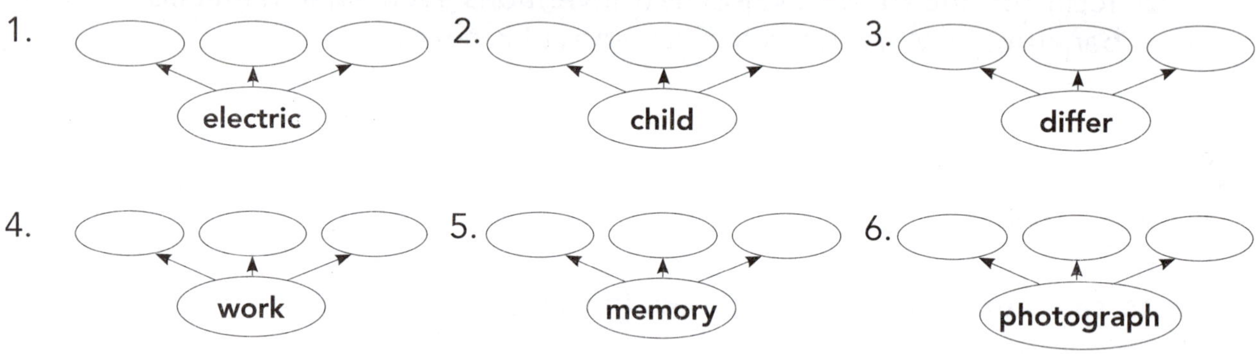

Grammar

active and passive voice

Read these sentences.

Edison hired Tesla to improve many of the machines he had invented.

Tesla was hired by Edison to improve many of the machines he had invented.

In the first sentence, the subject *Edison* is performing the action, *hired*. It is in the **active voice**.

In the second sentence, the subject *Tesla* is receiving the action, *was hired*. The sentence is in the **passive voice**.

When the doer of the action in a sentence is the subject, it is said to be in the **active voice**. When the recipient of the action of the verb is the subject, the sentence is said to be in the **passive voice**.

When a sentence is written in the passive voice, we add *by* before the doer of the action.

Examples: Tesla followed a strict routine. (*active voice*)

A strict routine was followed *by* Tesla. (*passive voice*)

Change the sentences from active voice to passive voice.

1. Bob closed the door.
2. The cat chased the mouse around the house.
3. The postman lost all my letters.
4. The brave firemen put out the fire.
5. The tourists were clicking photographs of the monument.
6. They were saying prayers for the earthquake victims.
7. The baker prepared a special cake for us.
8. The plumber repaired the clogged pipes in no time.

Study Skills

words with -*able* and -*ible*

Spelling

The pronunciation of the letters -*ible* and -*able* in words is often similar. Hence, their spelling may sometimes be confused. Words with -*able* are derived from other root words and make sense by themselves, while words with -*ible* do not make sense by themselves.

Examples: comfort + **able** = **comfortable** (the root word *comfort* makes sense by itself)

terr + **ible** = **terrible** (the word does not make any sense without the letters -*ible*)

Complete the words correctly with -*able* or -*ible*.

1. poss ________
2. notice ________
3. horr ________
4. ador ________
5. respons ________
6. change ________
7. revers ________
8. flex ________

Listening

listening for details

Listen to a passage on Inventors' Day and fill in the blanks.

1. Inventors' Day aims to pay ______________________ to all inventors.
2. Their inventions make the planet a ______________________.
3. Different countries have different ______________________.
4. Inventors' Day in most countries is usually a day ______________________.
5. In the USA, National Inventors' Day is celebrated on ______________________.
6. Edison held ______________________ patents in the USA alone.

Dictation

You will now listen to another short passage about Nikola Tesla and write it down. Each sentence will be repeated twice. Listen carefully and be careful not to make any spelling errors.

Speaking

interview

Work in pairs. Imagine that you are a newspaper reporter and your friend is Tesla. Enact a conversation where you interview Tesla about his life and work. Discuss the following topics in your interview, using information you have read about in the passage.

- role of his mother
- inventions
- working with Edison
- patents
- love for animals
- friends and investors
- life in New York

Useful words and phrases

Tell us about...
We heard that... is that true?
What projects...?
What do you enjoy doing other than...?
Which invention...?
If you were not a scientist...

Writing

email

Your school is organizing a science exhibition after two weeks. You would like to take part with your friend and present an exhibit. Write an email to your friend informing him/her about the exhibition and mentioning a few ideas for the exhibit. Invite your friend home for a brainstorming session.

Keep these points in mind while writing the email.

- The email ID of the recipient should be included correctly in the 'To' field.
- Mention the topic of the email in the 'Subject' field. It should be to the point.
- Do not mention the postal address of the sender or recipient in an email.

Self-Assessment

Now I can...

- o read and understand a biography about a scientist.
- o identify words related to science and make word families.
- o change sentences in the active voice to the passive voice.
- o spell words with *-able* and *-ible* correctly.
- o enact an interview and write an email.

Read at Leisure

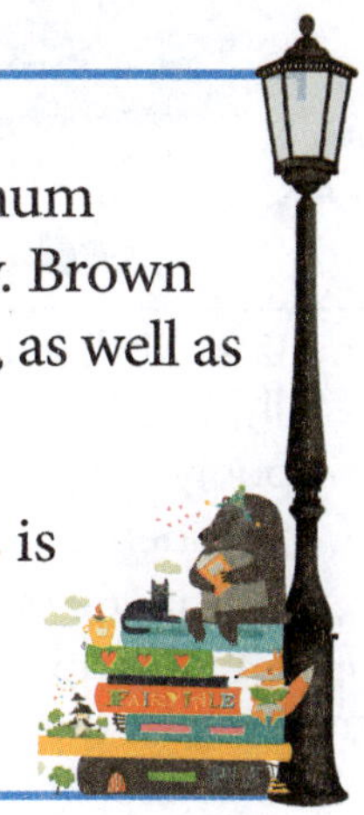

Barnum's Bones: This picture biography by Tracey E. Fern is about Barnum Brown, who was a scientist at the American Museum of Natural History. Brown had discovered the first documented skeleton of the Tyrannosaurus Rex, as well as most of the other dinosaurs on display there today.

Stories for Boys Who Dare To Be Different: This book by Ben Brooks is a compilation of 100 stories of extraordinary men, including Stephen Hawking, Barack Obama and Bill Gates, and their achievements.

18 Scientific Inquiry

Susan Blackaby

Reading

What do you think are the qualities required to be a scientist? Do you enjoy exploring and experimenting? Read this poem about the different steps of a scientific inquiry.

Scientists are like explorers[1],
using what they know and see
to **blaze a trail**[2] that, step by step,
will lead to new discoveries:

Formulate, **distil** and focus,
narrow down, define that **gist**,
determine **scope** and **pinpoint locus**–
this is your **hypothesis**.

Gather all the stuff you need,
to put in play the **machinations**.
Document the happenings–
these comprise your **observations**.

What things change and what things stick?
Record the outcomes and effects.
Don't **presume** and don't **predict**–[3]
collect the data: just the facts.

Combine the **concrete** things you see
with what you know and **trials** you test.
Interpretation is the key–[4]
results are where you end the **quest**.

formulate: work out a plan carefully
distil: purify
gist: main idea
scope: the range of a task
pinpoint: show exactly where something is
locus: the most important point associated with something
hypothesis: idea given as a possible explanation, which has not yet been proved
machinations: secret and complicated plans
document: (here) record
observations: (here) facts seen during an experiment
presume: believe something to be true
predict: guess what is going to happen in the future
concrete: (here) real or actual
trials: (here) experiments
Interpretation: opinion about what something means
quest: search

Common idioms and proverbs

2. **blaze a trail:** be the first to do or discover something that others follow

Literary terms

1. This is a **simile**, where the curious mind of a scientist is being compared to that of an explorer.
3. This is an example of **alliteration**, where the sound of 'p' is repeated in closely placed words.
4. This is a **metaphor**, where interpretation is being referred to as the most important aspect of the experiment, the 'key' to open the lock and find the results.

About the poet

Susan Blackaby (born 1953) is an American author and poet. She has written the picture books *Brownie Groundhog and the February Fox*, *Leo's Gift*, and an award-winning collection of poetry titled *Nest, Nook, and Cranny*.

Understanding the poem

A. Fill in the blanks.

1. The poet compares scientists to ________________ because they use what they ________________ and ________________.
2. The poet says that we should ________________ all the stuff we need and ________________ the happenings.
3. We should record the ________________ and ________________.
4. The poet asks us not to ________________ and ________________.
5. The poet says that ________________ is the key to finding ________________.

B. Answer these questions.

1. How do scientists make new discoveries?
2. How does one reach a hypothesis?
3. What comprises one's observations?
4. What should a scientist collect during an experiment?
5. What are the four key steps in a scientific process, according to the poem?

C. Answer the questions with reference to context.

1. *What things change and what things stick?/Record the outcomes and effects.*
   a. What does 'stick' mean here?
   b. What is the poet referring to in the first line?
   c. What is the difference between outcomes and effects?
2. *Interpretation is the key/Results are where you end the quest.*
   a. What is the 'quest' that the poet is referring to?
   b. What is the key to finding the 'results'?
   c. What should you combine to get the 'results'?

Life Skills and Values search for knowledge, understanding science

1. Why is it important for all of us to develop an attitude of 'scientific inquiry'? How will it help us explore new ideas?
2. Do you agree that science is all around us and a part of our everyday life? Give two examples to support your answer.

Vocabulary

idiomatic expressions

A. You have come across idioms in this poem. Match the idioms with their meanings.

Idioms	Meanings
1. cross your fingers	a. in trouble
2. raining cats and dogs	b. listening carefully
3. in hot water	c. very easy
4. a piece of cake	d. fold one finger across another in the hope of bringing good luck
5. all ears	e. deal with people threatening or attacking someone by using their own methods
6. fight fire with fire	f. raining heavily

B. Now fill in the blanks with the idioms from the previous exercise.

1. We had to cancel the picnic on Saturday as it was ______________
2. Annie did not study properly for the test. Now she is ______________
3. I was ______________ during the speech and heard each and every word of it.
4. ______________ and hope that you are selected for the school hockey team.
5. The soldiers decided to ______________ and attacked more fiercely.
6. The test was ______________ and I finished it earlier than expected.

Activity

writing a process

The poem refers to some important steps in the process of any scientific inquiry.

Read the poem again, and using the key words, create a flow chart of the process of inquiry that ends the 'quest'.

1. Scientists use ______________
2. This leads them to new ______________ ______________
3. They formulate ______________ and ______________
4. Keeping in mind the scope, ______________
5. They gather all the ______________ ______________
6. Then they document ______________ ______________
7. After that, they record ______________ ______________
8. Then they collect ______________ ______________
9. Then they combine ______________ ______________
10. Finally they find the result with ______________

Now I can... Self-Assessment

- enjoy a poem about the importance of developing a scientific mind.
- identify and use idioms in sentences.
- create a flow chart showing the sequence of a process.

Read at Leisure

Thinking Like a Scientist: This poem by Jennie Munson tells us to be curious and to learn by wondering, asking, testing and then drawing our own conclusions.

Science is Like Writing: This poem by Amy LV shows how scientific thought resembles poetic inspiration.

Project 3

A. You read about the creative world of the arts in 'The Concert' and 'Art is Hard'.

Work in pairs. Create a magazine advertisement for a concert by your favourite musician or band. An advertisement is similar to a poster, but it can include more detail.

Your advertisement should have the following elements.

- Main visual, related to the event
- A catchy phrase or sentence to draw the reader's attention. This should capture the main idea of the advertisement and act as an invitation to the event.
- Featuring artist/band
- The date and the venue
- Price of tickets and where they may be collected from
- Social media links, if any
- Contact details

You can refer to the sample poster before creating your own.

B. You have read about the groundbreaking inventions of Nikola Tesla. Now, find out the interesting stories behind these inventions. Write about them in a few lines each. Create a project file.

1. ball point pen	2. potato chips	3. zipper

4. Play-Doh	5. paper clip	6. Post-it

Literary Genres and Terms

Literary Genres

The stories and poems which you have read in this book are of various types. The following are some common kinds.

Prose

A **fable** is a story with a moral lesson at the end. In fables, animals, plants and non-living things often speak like humans.

A **fairy tale** is a story which has magical events and creatures like fairies, elves and goblins.

A **short story** narrates a tale that is only a few pages long.

A **folktale** is a story common among people who come from the same background. It is usually passed on in the form of an oral tale.

Humour is a type of literature which makes people laugh. A humorous story often has fun and excitement as its main elements.

Mythology includes traditional stories about gods that were told by people to explain natural events like lightning, and night and day.

Non-fiction is a type of literature that is based on real events rather than imaginary ones.

A **graphic story** is a story that is presented in comic-strip format.

An **adventure** is a type of story or book which has a lot of action, danger, risk and excitement.

Mystery is a genre of fiction that deals with the solution of a crime or the uncovering of secrets.

A **biography** is the story of a person's life, written by someone else.

A **fantasy** is a story or a novel which has a strange or other-worldly setting or characters. It often involves magic and supernatural creatures.

A **novel** is a long prose narrative that deals with human experiences in an imaginative way. It has a plot which shows the journeys of its various characters, and also explores their personalities in detail.

Poetry

A **nonsense poem** is a light-hearted, rhyming poem with characters in unusual situations. In such poems, everyday things are often described in an unusual way.

A **lyric poem** is a short poem whose main purpose is to express emotions or a state of mind. It does not depict actions or events.

Literary Terms

Literary terms include common figures of speech. These are the various techniques writers use to convey their message.

A **simile** is a figure of speech in which someone or something is compared to a very different person or thing using *as* or *like*. **Example:** He is as strong as an ox.

Alliteration is the use of the same letter or sound at the beginning of words in a sentence, especially in poetry. **Example:** Three grey geese were grazing in a green field.

Onomatopoeia is the use of words whose pronunciation is similar to the sounds they represent. **Examples:** thump, whoosh, swish

Personification is a way of imagining non-living things or abstract ideas as human beings with thoughts, actions and emotions. **Example:** The glass danced up and down on the table.

A **metaphor** is a figure of speech in which a person or thing is compared to another, otherwise unrelated person or thing by stating that they are the same in a particular way. **Example:** Pamela is the apple of her father's eye.

Imagery is the use of descriptive language to create pictures or images in the minds of readers. It appeals to the five senses. **Example:** It was a dark and stormy night.

Repetition is the use of the same word or phrase at intervals to give stress on a particular idea. **Example:** Listen to the words of wisdom,/Listen to the words of warning

Refrain is the repeated use of a line in different stanzas of a poem to create rhyme. **Example:** What does he plant who plants a tree?/He plants a friend of sun and sky ... What does he plant who plants a tree?/He plants cool shade and tender rain